OUR SACRED TEXTS
Discovering the Jewish Classics

by Ellen Singer
with
Bernard M. Zlotowitz

UAHC Press
New York, New York

To Don

Library of Congress Cataloging-in-Publication Data

Singer, Ellen
Our sacred texts: discovering the Jewish classics/by Ellen Singer with Bernard M. Zlotowitz.
p.   cm.
Includes biographical references.
Summary: Explores such Jewish sacred texts as the Hebrew Bible, the Talmud, the Midrash, and medieval Jewish literature; discusses responsa and the prayer book; and features learning activities throughout.
ISBN 0-8074-0479-9 (alk. paper): $8.00
1. Judaism—Sacred books—Introductions—Juvenile literature.
2. Jewish religious education—Textbooks for children.
[1. Judaism—Sacred books. 2. Jewish religious education.]
I. Zlotowitz, Bernard M. II. Title.
BM496.5.S55   1992
296.1—dc20   92-16438 √
                                                                      CIP
                                                                      AC

This book is printed on acid-free paper
Copyright © 1992 by the UAHC Press
Manufactured in the United States of America
10 9 8 7 6 5 4 3 2 1

CONTENTS

ACKNOWLEDGMENTS

Writing this book has been a tremendously challenging as well as fulfilling experience. I would like to acknowledge the support and assistance provided me by certain key people. Thanks to Aron Hirt-Manheimer, who opened the door for me. To Michael Freedman, Ben Koerner, and David Krivit, I give thanks for serving as my living laboratory. Their influence and input touch every page of the book. The keen, scholarly eye of Rabbi Bernard M. Zlotowitz has been invaluable. His participation in this undertaking adds considerably to its credibility and stature.

This book has also benefited from the constructive guidance of its reading committee: Rabbi Howard I. Bogot, Robin L. Eisenberg, Gail Teicher Fellus, Niles Goldstein, Constance R. Reiter, Dr. Lenore Sandel, Lesley M. Silverstone, Rabbi Jonathan A. Stein, and Robert E. Tornberg. I also extend my gratitude to Annette Abramson for her fine copyediting, to William Cwiekalo for his design of this volume, and to Stuart L. Benick for his careful guidance of this book to its finished form.

My editor, David P. Kasakove, supported me through every word of the writing process. Every writer should be fortunate enough to have a kind, thoughtful, and insightful editor like David.

I want to thank my husband, Don, whose encouragement and love kept me going. And, when I needed it most, he made me laugh.

The Discovery Begins

Y ou are about to begin a journey into the world of
Jewish sacred texts.   As with any trip, you will
encounter some things that are familiar and
many that are not. On your journey you will make dis-
coveries, uncover hidden meanings, and learn some
things about your heritage that you didn't know before.
To get you started on this journey it may be useful to
give you a "map" of where you are going.

In this book, you will learn that the word Torah has many meanings. It is a scroll like the ones you have seen in the *Aron Hakodesh* אֲרוֹן הַקֹּדֶשׁ ("Holy Ark") in your temple sanctuary.* Torah is the word for the first section of the Jewish Bible, the Five Books of Moses. It can be used to mean the entire Jewish Bible including the Prophets and the Writings. Finally, Torah can mean any book of Jewish law or rabbinic commentary. Torah is all of Jewish learning!

The early religion and ancient history of the Jewish people are recorded in the Jewish Bible. We have always treasured this account of our beginnings. Our ongoing commitment to the Torah has linked us to past and future generations of Jews. Each new generation of Jews has been strengthened by interpreting and expanding the laws and lessons of the Torah to fit the changing needs of the times. These expansions and interpretations were compiled into a series of different books that are part of what we call our sacred texts. As you know, sacred means holy. We call our texts "sacred" because they include laws and teachings designed to help us lead holy lives. The first sacred text you will encounter on your travels is the Torah. But, as you will soon discover, there are many other sacred texts that are part of our living heritage.

You will begin your journey by traveling to two very different worlds. First, you will stop off in the ancient Israel that existed over 1,900 years ago. The second stop on your itinerary will be Nazi-occupied Poland during World War II. While many centuries and thousands of miles separate these two stops, the Jews you will meet are united by their commitment to our sacred texts and their willingness to risk their lives to preserve them.

Rabbi Akiva: A Story of Courage and Faith

Can you imagine a wife encouraging her husband to go off to study, even though it meant leaving her for years at a time? How about a forty-year-old man changing his career and starting on a whole new path? Well, Akiva ben Joseph's wife, Rachel, not only encouraged him to go and study, she insisted he do it. Akiva was a poor, illiterate shepherd, who lived in the Land of Israel during the first and second centuries of the common era (about 50-135 C.E.). At about age forty, he went off to study Torah. First he had to learn to read Hebrew! Despite his late start, Akiva became one of the most important and respected rabbis in Jewish history.

Rabbi Akiva boldly continued to teach Torah despite Roman prohibitions against Jewish study.

Life was not easy for Rabbi Akiva and his fellow Jews. The Romans who ruled the Land of Israel restricted their actions and made life difficult. On top of the ruins of the holy Jewish Temple the Romans built a temple to their gods and converted Jerusalem into a Roman city.

The Romans enacted laws that limited the practice of Judaism and prohibited the teaching of Torah. Akiva chose to ignore the Roman laws. He boldly continued to teach Torah and even did so openly. When asked how he could teach in defiance of the Roman edict, Rabbi Akiva told the following story:

One day, as a fox was walking along the shore, he saw fish darting back and forth in the water.

"What are you fleeing from?" the fox asked them.

"The fishermen's nets," the fish replied.

"Why not come out onto the shore?" suggested the sly fox. "Once your ancestors and mine lived side by side upon the land."

But the fish replied, "If we are in danger in the sea where we live, how much greater will be the danger in a place that spells our death!"

"So it is with us," explained Akiva. "If we are in danger when we study Torah, which is our Tree of Life, imagine how much greater our danger will be if we follow the Roman prohibitions and no longer cling to Torah!"

Eventually, Akiva was imprisoned and sentenced to die for teaching Torah. On the day of Akiva's execution, the Romans took him while he was reciting the morning prayers. As Akiva was about to be executed, his voice rang out the words of the *Shema*, "Hear, O Israel: *Adonai* is our God, *Adonai* is One! And you shall love *Adonai* your God with all your heart and with all your being and with all your might."

Akiva's students heard their beloved teacher speak these words, and they cried out, "Master, how can you recite these words, even now?"

Akiva answered, "All my life I wondered how I could fulfill the commandment to love God with all my being. I wondered if I would ever be able to give up my entire being to serve God. Now that I have the opportunity, should I not grab it?" In both life and death Rabbi Akiva was a model of devotion to God, Torah, and Judaism.

The Secret of the Yanov Torah

The year is 1941. The place is Yanov, a Nazi work camp in Eastern Europe. Returning from a visit outside the camp, Moshe the tailor anxiously waits while the guards of the Yanov camp examine his identification papers. One suspicious move and he might be searched. The longer Moshe waits, the greater the pounding of his heart against the parchment wrapped tightly around his body. He stands stiffly as one of the guards rises, circles the table, grips Moshe's shoulders, and pushes him to the ground. Blackout.

When Moshe awakens in the barracks, he feels a deep pain in his chest. He remembers his mission and, with frantic fingers, tears at the buttons of his shirt. The sacred parchment is still there, wrapped around his body. The Torah has entered Yanov!

What exactly was Moshe's mission? Why was it so important to bring a Torah into Yanov? This is the story behind the secret of the Yanov Torah: In 1941 all the able-bodied men and women of Moshe's home town of Lvov were forced into a Nazi work camp in nearby Yanov.

Even in Yanov, a Nazi work camp, Jews risked their lives to study Torah.

One day, much to all the prisoners' surprise, a group of men was allowed to return home for twenty-four hours. During the visit a remarkable story was revealed: Every day, religious services were secretly conducted in the barracks of the Yanov camp. Now, they wanted a Torah.

Back and forth the elders of the community argued the pros and cons of trying to meet this request. What if the Nazis found the Torah? What if all future visits were cancelled? What would be the punishment if the plan was discovered? Finally, a decision was made. One of the Torah scrolls that had been buried in the Jewish cemetery was dug up, separated into pieces, and smuggled into the camp piece by piece. The Jews of the Yanov camp were starved, beaten, and worked until they dropped. Yet somehow they did not lose their faith or their courage. The Yanov Torah gave them the strength to go on.

In the weeks after the liberation, the survivors forgot about their Torah. All of them, that is, except for Moshe. By questioning former Yanov inmates, he was able to find all the pieces, hidden in the hollow rails of the bedposts and in holes in the floor, and carefully restore the Torah. Months later, at a meeting of the Yanov survivors, the lovingly restored Yanov Torah was presented to the oldest Jewish survivor of the Yanov camp, who still lived in Lvov. This man embraced the Torah, and then he kissed it. "I cherish this honor. When I die, our Torah shall be entrusted to the oldest survivor of the Yanov camp." From that day on, whenever the oldest survivor of Yanov died, the Torah was passed on to the next oldest survivor.

But the story of this special Torah was not over. In 1980, a Jewish doctor and his family were making plans to leave the USSR. Before leaving, the doctor visited an ailing, elderly man. This man was not only the oldest survivor of Yanov he was the *last* one. The old man told the doctor the story of the Yanov Torah. Then he handed the Torah to the doctor and said, "Take the Torah, take it with you to America. In America it will live!"

When the doctor and his family arrived at the Russian border, they were forced to pay all their money for the "extra baggage," the Torah. They arrived in America penniless but free and secure in the knowledge that they had fulfilled their promise to keep the Yanov Torah alive.

ACTIVITIES

The story Rabbi Akiva tells about the fox and the fish includes many elements that have symbolic meanings. Match the elements from Rabbi Akiva's story (column A) with the appropriate symbolic meaning (column B).

A	B
the fish	the Romans
the sea	the Jews
the fox	the Torah

Put an "A" next to the words that you think describe Rabbi Akiva. Put a "Y" next to the words you think describe the Jews of the Yanov camp.

___ courageous   ___ foolhardy   ___ committed

___ crazy   ___ extraordinary   ___ heroic

Complete the following sentences.

1. Rabbi Akiva continued to teach Torah in defiance of Roman laws because

   _____

   _____

   _____

2. Moshe the tailor volunteered for the risky job of bringing the Torah into the Yanov camp because _____

   _____

   _____

3. The Soviet doctor agreed to take the Yanov Torah to America, even though it cost him all the money he had with him because _____

   _____

   _____

4. The actions of Akiva, Moshe, and the Soviet doctor are similar because

   _____

   _____

   _____

5. Romans and Nazis took away the rights of Jews to study Torah openly because

   _____

   _____

   _____

Introduction: Summary

As Jews, we show our commitment to Torah not only through studying but also, when necessary, by taking risks to preserve Torah and our right to observe the laws and rituals described in it. Jewish history consists of many stories of courage like those of Rabbi Akiva and the Jews of Yanov.

Having begun your journey into a new world of learning, you will encounter an amazing collection of classic Jewish texts that we call sacred. These texts are holy, unique, and set apart from everyday books. One of your goals will be to discover why each of these texts is worthy of the label "sacred."

In the next unit, you will learn more about the significance of Torah and explore some of its contents and meanings.

Gustave Doré, France, 1865

"Before the creation of the world, God created the Torah."

8

The Torah

About This Unit: In the Introduction you read about two Jews who treasured Torah so deeply that they risked their lives to protect their right to study Torah and to observe the laws and customs included in it. In this unit when we refer to *the* Torah it will mean the Five Books of Moses. What exactly is in the Torah? Where did it come from? Who wrote it? You will explore these questions and begin to form your own answers.

What Is the Torah?

Jewish legend states that, before the creation of the world, God created the Torah. Why? So that God could use the teachings of the Torah as a blueprint for how all creation should behave and interact. This legend teaches us that the Torah is more than a precious object. Through reading and studying the Torah, we learn how to behave as Jews and as human beings. In fact, the Hebrew word *Torah* תּוֹרָה actually means "instruction." The stories, the narration, the laws, and the poetry included in the Torah are all aimed at teaching. They teach us about the beginnings of the world, the early history of the Jewish people, and life in the world of ancient Israel. Taken altogether the Torah is the framework around which we build our lives.

The Torah is important not only to Jews. It is also important to the world at large. The Torah serves as the foundation for two of the world's other major religions, Christianity and Islam. It is considered a classic of world literature. And there are more translations of the Bible than of any other major literary work.

Many of the teachings of the Torah, especially those dealing with respect for others and acting fairly towards one another, are accepted by Jews and non-Jews alike. *For example*: The Torah teaches "You shall not commit robbery" (*Vayikra*/Leviticus 19:13); "You shall not insult the deaf, or place a stumbling block before the blind" (*Vayikra*/Leviticus 19:14); "Love your neighbor as yourself" (*Vayikra*/Leviticus 19:18); "You shall rise before the aged and show respect to the old." (*Vayikra*/ Leviticus 19:32)

Another example of the Torah's wide-ranging appeal and influence is found in the quote chosen for the Liberty Bell. Engraved on this important American symbol is the biblical verse "Proclaim liberty throughout the land for all its inhabitants." These words actually come from the third book of the Torah, *Vayikra*/Leviticus 25:10.

The Many Names for the Torah

Understanding the Torah begins with looking at its structure and organization. Another name for the Torah is the Five Books of Moses, a name honoring our great teacher and leader. Tradition states that Moses acted as a representative for all the Jewish people when he received the Torah at Mount Sinai. The English titles of each of the Five Books of Moses are: Genesis, Exodus, Leviticus, Numbers, and Deuteronomy. These names come from the Greek translation of the Torah. Each title represents the main theme covered by each of the five books.

The Torah is also referred to by the Hebrew name *Chumash* חוּמָשׁ, which means "five." The Hebrew names of the books of the *Chumash* are taken from the first word or words of each book. Their names, their meanings, and a brief look at their contents follow:

1. Bereshit בְּרֵאשִׁית means "When [God] began." *Bereshit* focuses on the beginnings of the world and the beginnings of the Jewish people.

2. Shemot שְׁמוֹת means "Names." The first lines of this book list the names of Jacob's family members who accompanied him to Egypt. *Shemot* tells of the Jewish people's life as slaves, the redemption from slavery, and the revelation at Mount Sinai when God gave us the Torah.

3. Vayikra וַיִּקְרָא means "And [*Adonai*] called." This book's main focus is on directions for sacrifices and the proper ritual behavior of the priests.

4. Bemidbar בְּמִדְבַּר means "In the desert." This is a reference to the Children of Israel's years of wandering in the desert, which is the central theme of this book.

5. Devarim דְּבָרִים means "Words." In *Devarim* Moses repeats the instructions, laws, warnings, and blessings found in the earlier books of the Torah. The final chapter describes the death of Moses.

ACTIVITY

The Five Books of the Torah

Match the Hebrew name of each book of the Torah (column A) to the proper English name (column B) and to the correct description of the book's contents (column C).

A	B	C
Bereshit בְּרֵאשִׁית	Deuteronomy	years of wandering in the desert
Shemot שְׁמוֹת	Leviticus	repetition of all the laws; the death of Moses
Vayikra וַיִקְרָא	Genesis	beginnings of the world and of the Jewish people
Bemidbar בְּמִדְבַּר	Exodus	sacrifices and priestly behavior
Devarim דְּבָרִים	Numbers	slavery, redemption, and revelation

Who Wrote the Torah?

How the Torah, the Five Books of Moses, came to be written is a question with many different answers. The explanation given in the Torah itself says, "When God finished speaking with Moses on Mount Sinai, God gave Moses the two tablets of the Pact, stone tablets written with the finger of God." (*Shemot*/Exodus 31:18) The Torah also tells us that God told Moses all the laws the Jewish people were to follow. Moses recorded all these laws as well as all that had happened to the Jews up until the time of his death.

Some Jews believe that the Jewish people received the Torah just as it is described above. These Jews believe that the entire Torah is the revealed word of God. Moses was a messenger and did not include any of his own ideas or thoughts. According to this approach, it is okay for a Jew to question and search for the underlying meaning of the Torah, but it is not okay to reject beliefs and *mitzvot* מִצְוֹת ("commandments") either because they are not clearly understandable or because they are no longer relevant. Jews who believe this way encourage studying and examining the Torah but also believe in the obligation to follow all of God's *mitzvot.**

Other Jews believe that God spoke the words of the Torah, and these words were recorded not only by

* Mitzvot *(plural for mitzvah) means "commandments." The commandments of Judaism come from the Torah. The meaning of some mitzvot are easy to understand because they are stated clearly. For example: You shall not murder (Exodus 20:13); You shall rise before the aged and show respect to the old. (Leviticus 19:32) Other mitzvot are not stated as clearly. It is the task of rabbis and scholars to try to understand and explain the best way to follow these mitzvot. For example: Remember the Sabbath day and keep it holy (Exodus 20:8); Seven days you shall eat unleavened bread. (Exodus 13:6) After reading these mitzvot in the Torah, we might ask: "What actions must we do to keep the Sabbath holy?" "What are the ingredients of this unleavened bread? How do we make it?" The answers to these questions show us how to perform these mitzvot.*

76.67. *From the collection of Hebrew Union College Skirball Museum*

Moses and the Ten Commandments. *Lithograph, 19th century.*

Moses but also by different men and women over the ages. This approach permits reinterpreting the Torah and the *mitzvot* based on changes in lifestyles. Any changes in Jewish laws made to update and modernize them are guided by a desire to hold on to tradition and to make room for change to keep Judaism alive. The job of studying and working out these changes belongs to a committee of respected scholars and rabbis.

Still other Jews believe that, while the Torah is indeed a very holy book and the basis of Judaism, it was written by human beings who were inspired by God. In this light, the Torah is really a record of people's evolving ideas about how to best serve God. Looking at the Torah more as human creation than God revelation means that it is easier to change and reinterpret it. Of course, a great deal of what the Jews wrote years ago still sounds right today, especially the moral and ethical laws that teach us how to behave towards our fellow human beings. Therefore, it is important to study the Torah with the greatest respect. But, when we encounter laws that no longer apply to the way we live today, we may decide that these laws do not describe how we can best serve God in our own times.

Jews who view the Torah this way suggest that the traditional *mitzvot* serve as a guide rather than an unchangeable rule. The *halachah* הֲלָכָה ("system of Jewish law") has a vote in deciding how we are to live and act but not a veto. To put it another way, all the ethical and moral laws in the Torah stand firm. But, in the area of ritual, changes are allowed when they are made and supported by the community.

What Do the Scholars Say?

The question "Who wrote the Torah?" is not a new one. It is one that rabbis and scholars have wrestled and struggled with throughout the centuries. Their answers have led to many related questions. *For example*: If the Torah came directly from God, does this mean only God can change it? Can Jews living today, who think and live differently from Jews in earlier times, interpret the Torah in ways that make sense for modern times? Below are the answers to some of these questions, given by respected, well-known Jews. Each quotation is followed by the name of the author and the dates of his life.

1. The Torah was precisely transmitted from God and no one else. To the Torah . . . nothing must be added nor anything taken from it, as it is written in *Devarim*/Deuteronomy 13:1, "neither add to it nor take away from it." (Maimonides, also known as Rambam, 1135-1204) *

2. The Torah is intrinsically perfect; it requires no external evidence for the truths it teaches. (Abraham ibn Ezra, 1092-1167)

3. The Torah is eternal, but its explanation is to be made by the spiritual leaders of Judaism . . . in accordance with the age. (Ba'al Shem Tov, 1700-1760)

4. Any interpretation that conforms to reason must be correct. (Sa'adiah Gaon, 882-942)

* *Many famous rabbis are known by more than one name. Some had names that their parents gave them, and names that were shortened versions of their longer names. For example: Moses ben Maimon was known by the general public, as well as by his fellow Jews, as RaMBaM (Rabbi Moses Ben Maimon).*

13

5. The person who meditates over words of Torah is constantly finding new meaning in them. (Rabbi Shelomoh ben Isaac, also known as Rashi, 1040-1105)

6. There are innumerable ways of explaining the Torah. (Nachmanides, also known as Ramban, 1194-1270)

7. There is no other Jewish religion but that taught by the Torah and confirmed by history and tradition and sunk into the conscience of all of the Jewish people. (Rabbi Solomon Schechter, 1847-1915)

8. We must insist upon this one article of faith, "I believe in the revelation of God and the God of revelation." (Rabbi Isaac Mayer Wise, 1819-1900)

9. The Torah is the most precious legacy our forbearers bequeathed to us. But, to inherit it, we must be more than just its passive recipients. We must earn it for ourselves by turning to it over and over again. (Rabbi Alexander M. Schindler, 1925-   )

ACTIVITIES

Who Said What?

The following statements restate the quotes above.
Match each statement with the quote it explains. To the left of each statement, write the number of the matching quote and the name of the author.

_____ There are so many possible interpretations of the Torah that they are impossible to count.

_____ Serious reading and studying of the Torah always leads to finding new meaning in the words.

_____ The Torah by its nature is perfect.

_____ All of Jewish religion comes from the Torah and has been reinforced all throughout the history of the Jewish people.

_____ The Torah has meaning for all Jews for all ages, but it is up to the spiritual leaders of a specific time to decide its meaning for that period in history.

_____ The Torah is the most precious gift given to us by our ancestors. To be fully deserving of this gift we must read, study, and explore all of it.

_____ Logic and reason are solid tools when trying to understand the Torah.

_____ The Torah came directly from God. We are not allowed to add or to subtract from the words of the Torah.

_____ The central belief of Judaism must be belief in the God who gave us the Torah at Mount Sinai.

What Do You Believe?

As you can see, there are almost as many ways to understand the Torah as there are Jews. Below are statements taken from the paragraphs above. Read these statements. After each one, circle either "I agree" or "I disagree" and *explain* why.

1. Jews are obligated to follow all of God's *mitzvot* whether or not the reasons behind them are clear. I agree/I disagree _____

   _____

2. When we encounter laws that no longer apply to the way we live today, we may decide that these laws do not describe how we can best serve God in our own times. I agree/I disagree _____

   _____

3. God spoke the words of the Torah, and these words were recorded by men and women. I agree/I disagree _____

   _____

Unit One: Summary

In this section, you reviewed the structure of the Torah. You learned of the different beliefs about its origin and interpretation. Common to all these views is the belief that the Torah stands at the center of Judaism. In the next chapter, you will begin to explore the contents of the Torah, starting with *Bereshit*/Genesis.

Prague Bible. *Bereshit, 1518.*

CHAPTER 1

BERESHIT/GENESIS:
The Making of the Covenant

About This Chapter: As you have already learned, Torah means "teaching" or "instruction." Our rabbis teach us that we can learn something from each and every Torah passage. The passages you will study in this chapter describe the special relationship known as the covenant that exists between God and the Jewish people. As you read each passage, try to figure out what the Torah is trying to teach you about the covenant.

Bereshit/Genesis: Beginnings

Bereshit/Genesis, the first book of the Torah, is about beginnings. In the first chapters of *Bereshit*/Genesis, the creation stories tell of the beginning of the world. From the story of Noah we learn about a second beginning of the world, which takes place after the Flood. Next, the story of the Tower of Babel explains the beginnings of many different languages and peoples throughout the world. All of these are followed by the beginning of the Jewish people, told through the stories of Abraham, Sarah, Isaac, Rebecca, Jacob, Leah, Rachel, and their families.* The early foundations of the Jewish people are set when God establishes a special connection with these important leaders. In these pages you will read about the unfolding of this relationship.

The Special Relationship between God and the Jewish People

The particular Torah passages given here illustrate the Jewish people's special connection with God. In *Bereshit*, God initiates the relationship with the Jewish nation. Read on to find out how it was established.

Abraham

Abraham is one of the first people mentioned in the Torah whose story includes some details about his life and personal history. What do we know about Abraham? His birthplace is probably the city of Ur in Mesopotamia, which is now Iraq. According to the Torah, as an adult, Abraham travels with his wife, Sarah, his father, Terah, and his nephew, Lot, to a

* Patriarch and Matriarch
The head of a family is called a patriarch (from the Latin word pater, *for "father") or a matriarch (from the Latin word* mater, *for "mother"). Abraham, Isaac, and Jacob are called the patriarchs of the Jewish people; their wives, Sarah, Rebecca, Leah, and Rachel are called the matriarchs of the Jewish people. Why do you think they have these titles?*

Abraham and Isaac on the Way to the Place of Sacrifices. *Ephraim Moses Lilien, Germany, circa 1910. Magazine illustration.*

place named Haran. Abraham makes a living as a shepherd. Like many other people of his day, Abraham and his family are seminomads. They stay in one place until they need to move on in search of additional grazing lands for their animals. While the Torah does not give us the dates of Abraham's life, scholars have figured out that he lived about 1800 B.C.E. In Haran, Abraham receives a call from God. This moment marks the beginning of Abraham's relationship with God. The covenant, the unique relationship between God and the Jewish people, is first established when God speaks to Abraham.

In *Bereshit* 12 you will read about the first communication between God and Abraham. After carefully reading these verses, answer the questions that follow.

1] *Adonai* said to Abram [later known as Abraham], "Go forth from your native land and from your father's house to the land that I will show you. **2]** I will make of you a great nation,/ And I will bless you;/ I will make your name great,/ And you shall be a blessing./ **3]** I will bless those who bless you/ And curse those that curse you;/ And all the families of the earth/ Shall bless themselves by you." **4]** Abram went forth as *Adonai* had commanded him, and Lot went with him. Abram was seventy-five years old when he left Haran. **5]** Abram took his wife Sarai [later known as Sarah] and his brother's son Lot, and all the wealth that they had amassed, and the persons that they had acquired in Haran; and they set out for the land of Canaan.

(Bereshit 12:1-5)*

☆ *Whenever a quotation is taken from the Torah, it is followed by information that tells you where in the Torah these words can be found. For example: When you read Genesis 12:1-5, you will know that Genesis is the name of the book of the Torah; 12 is the number of the chapter of the book; and 1-5 are the numbers of the verses. Find Genesis 12:1-5 in a printed copy of the Torah.*

ACTIVITIES

God's first words to Abraham were "Go forth from your native land and from your father's house to the land that I will show you." Which of the following statements do you think best describes the message behind these words?

_____ You must separate yourself from your past in order to carry out this plan I have for your future.

_____ The first test of your trust in Me will be for you to leave all that is familiar to you – your homeland, your family – and go to a new, unknown place.

_____ Do as I say and do not question My plan for you.

Write your own description.

_____

_____

Which of the following does God promise Abraham?

___ a large family   ___ the leadership of an important nation

___ wealth   ___ lots of descendants   ___ fame

What does God ask Abraham to promise in return?

_____

_____

Bereshit 17 reports another communication between God and Abraham. Compare the above passage from *Bereshit* 12 with the one you are about to read. Look for differences in the relationship as described in the two passages.

1] When Abram was ninety-nine years old, *Adonai* appeared to Abram and said to him, "I am *El Shaddai*. Walk in My ways and be blameless. **2]** I will establish My covenant between Me and you, and I will make you exceedingly numerous."*

3] Abram threw himself on his face, as God spoke to him further, **4]** "As for Me, this is My covenant with you: You shall be the father of a multitude of nations. **5]** And you shall no longer be called Abram, but your name shall be Abraham, for I make you the father of a multitude of nations. **6]** I will make you exceedingly fertile, and make nations of you; and kings shall come forth from you. **7]** I will maintain My covenant between Me and you, and your offspring to come, as an everlasting covenant throughout the ages, to be God to you and to your offspring to come. **8]** I give the land you sojourn in to you and your offspring to come, all the land of Canaan, as an everlasting possession. I will be their God."

9] God further said to Abraham, "As for you, you and your offspring to come throughout the ages shall keep My covenant. **10]** Such shall be the covenant between Me and you and your offspring to follow which you shall keep: every male among you shall be circumcised. **11]** You shall circumcise the flesh of your foreskin, and that shall be the sign of the covenant between Me and you. **12]** And throughout the generations, every male among you shall be circumcised at the age of eight days. As for the homeborn slave and the one bought from an outsider who is not of your offspring, **13]** they must be circumcised, homeborn and purchased alike. Thus shall My covenant be marked in your flesh as an everlasting pact."

(*Bereshit* 17:1-13)

The Hebrew word for covenant is berit בְּרִית. *In Genesis 17:9-14, God reiterates the covenant between Abraham and his offspring (that is, the Jewish people) and adds that, as a sign of the covenant, "You shall circumcise the flesh of your foreskin . . . and throughout the generations, every male among you shall be circumcised at the age of eight days." The act of ritual circumcision known as* berit milah *continues to be performed to this day. How is the continuing practice of* berit milah *a symbol of the ongoing covenant between God and the Jewish people?*

📖 **ACTIVITIES**

Which of the promises made by God in *Bereshit* 17:1-13 was *not* mentioned in *Bereshit* 12?

___ the leadership of a large nation   ___ many descendants

___ royal descendants   ___ land

ACTIVITIES (CONTINUED)

What does God insist Abraham do as his part of their special relationship?

_____

_____

In *Bereshit* 17, the special relationship between God and the Jewish people is given a name. What is it called? _____

Isaac

Isaac was the son of Abraham and Sarah. We read in the Torah that, after many years of hoping and praying for a child, Abraham and Sarah receive the news from messengers of God that their prayers will be answered. Abraham and Sarah, who now are both old, laugh with joy and disbelief. When the excited parents finally see their baby, they name him Isaac, which means "laughter," as a reminder of their first reaction to the news of their son's birth.

The Torah provides us with little information on Isaac's life before his marriage to Rebecca. We do know that, when Isaac is a young man, Abraham is commanded to sacrifice Isaac as a test of his faith in God. Just as Abraham raises his hand to carry out the command, an angel stops him and provides a ram to sacrifice in place of Isaac. We also know that as an adult Isaac lives the life of a seminomad. But his movements are confined to a relatively small area around Beer-sheba, in the southern half of modern Israel. In addition, we know that Isaac earns a living tending cattle and sheep, as well as doing farming.

Isaac marries his cousin Rebecca at age forty. They, too, long for children for many years before they give birth to twins, Jacob and Esau. (More on the twins later!) Sometime after the twins grow up, famine strikes in Canaan. God forbids Isaac from going down to Egypt in search of food. Instead Isaac stays in Canaan but moves from the Beer-sheba area to Gerar, an area ruled by Philistines.

Isaac's story in the Torah, unlike that of his father, Abraham, or his son, Jacob, is short on details. We are not told how he reacts to almost being sacrificed or to learning that his mother has died. What *we are told very clearly* is that Isaac represents the first step towards fulfilling God's promise to Abraham—that he will be the father of a great nation. Isaac serves as the bridge between Abraham and Jacob.

In *Bereshit* 26, God repeated to Isaac the *berit* ("covenant") that he had made with Isaac's father, Abraham:

1] There was a famine in the land—aside from the previous famine that had occurred in the days of Abraham—and Isaac went to Abimelech, king of the Philistines, in Gerar. **2]** *Adonai* had appeared to him and said, "Do not go down to Egypt; stay in the land which I point out to you. **3]** Reside in this land, and I will be with you and bless you; I will give all these lands to you and to your offspring, fulfilling the oath that I swore to your father Abraham. **4]** I will make your descendants as numerous as the stars of heaven, and give to your descendants all these lands, so that all the nations of the earth shall bless themselves by your offspring— **5]** inasmuch as Abraham obeyed Me and kept My charge: My commandments, My laws, and My teachings.

(Bereshit 26:1-5)

ACTIVITIES

What is the first thing God commands Isaac to do?

_____

_____

In return for following God's command which of the following is Isaac promised?

___ children   ___ land   ___ millions of descendants

___ respect   ___ wealth   ___ leadership of a great nation

There is a new element mentioned in the *berit* ("covenant") as it is described in *Bereshit* 26. Compare *Bereshit* 17:1-13 with *Bereshit* 26:1-5 to figure out what Abraham and now Isaac have to obey and keep as their part of the *berit*.

_____

_____

Jacob

In the Torah we read that Jacob and his twin brother, Esau, come into the world fighting and spend a lot of their early years at odds with each other. Esau possesses great skill as a hunter and enjoys the outdoors. He is favored by Isaac, their father. Jacob, a more mild mannered man, stays closer to home and is favored by Rebecca, their mother. Once, when Jacob cooks up a delicious stew, Esau comes home very hungry. As soon as Esau catches the aroma of this tasty dish, he quickly agrees to give up his birthright—his special rights as the firstborn son—in exchange for a steaming hot bowl of stew. Of course, Esau later regrets his hasty decision.

Jacob's Ladder. *Rembrandt van Rijn, etching, 1655.*

When their father, Isaac, is on his deathbed, Jacob once again outfoxes his brother Esau. This time he does so with the advice of his mother. Jacob appears before his father disguised as Esau. Blind Isaac is fooled and gives Jacob the blessing he had intended for Esau, the blessing for the firstborn. This blessing states that Jacob will be a great leader with power over others, even over his brother. When Esau discovers the trick, he is outraged. Jacob flees to escape his brother's rage.

The first night of his flight Jacob has an amazing dream in which God repeats the *berit* to him. This is the same *berit* that God earlier established with Abraham and Isaac.

The story of Jacob's amazing dream is found in *Bereshit* 28.

10] Jacob left Beer-sheba, and set out for Haran. **11]** He came upon a certain place and stopped there for the night, for the sun had set. Taking one of the stones of that place, he put it under his head and lay down in that place. **12]** He had a dream; a stairway was set on the ground and its top reached to the sky, and angels of God were going up and down on it. **13]** And *Adonai* was standing beside him and said, "I am *Adonai,* the God of your father Abraham and the God of Isaac: the ground on which you are lying I will give to you and to your offspring. **14]** Your descendants shall be as dust of the earth; you shall spread out to the west and to the east, to the north and to the south. All the families of the earth shall bless themselves by you and your descendants. **15]** Remember, I am with you: I will protect you wherever you go and will bring you back to this land. I will not leave you until I have done what I promised you."

16] Jacob awoke from his sleep and said, "Surely *Adonai* is present in this place, and I did not know it!" **17]** Shaken, he said, "How awesome is this place! This is none other than the abode of God, and that is the gateway to heaven." **18]** Early in the morning, Jacob took the stone that he had put under his head and set it up as a pillar and poured oil on the top of it. **19]** He named that site Bethel; but previously the name of the city had been Luz.

20] Jacob then made a vow, saying, "If God remains with me, if God protects me on this journey that I am making, and gives me bread to eat and clothing to wear, **21]** and if I return safe to my father's house—*Adonai* shall be my God."

(*Bereshit* 28:10-21)

Compare the *berit* as stated to Jacob, Isaac, and Abraham. Read the list of parts of the *berit* and check off which items were directly mentioned to each of the three leaders. For help in completing the activity, review the passages from *Bereshit* 12, 17, 26, and 28.

	Abraham	Isaac	Jacob
lots of descendants	_____	_____	_____
leadership of a great nation	_____	_____	_____
a great name (fame)	_____	_____	_____
royal descendants	_____	_____	_____
land	_____	_____	_____
circumcision	_____	_____	_____
obey God's laws	_____	_____	_____
respect from others	_____	_____	_____

Jacob's last words seem to indicate that if God fulfills God's end of the bargain then Jacob will fulfill his part. How do you react to this reasoning? If God made a *berit* with you, would you bargain with God? Explain your answer.

_____

_____

_____

"A *berit* ('covenant') is a special agreement made by two or more parties." Based on what you read in this chapter, prove this statement.

_____

_____

_____

How does the Torah teach in *all* the passages in this chapter that the *berit* binds not only Abraham, Isaac, and Jacob but all Jews?

_____

_____

_____

How does the *berit* fit into your life? Throughout time it has been the responsibility of every single Jew to keep up the *berit* with God. How should you act to fulfill your responsibilities of the covenant?

MY PERSONAL RESPONSES FOR FULFILLING THE BERIT

1. My responsibilities to myself are

    _____

    _____

2. My responsibilities to my family are

    _____

    _____

3. My responsibilities to my Jewish community are

    _____

    _____

4. My responsibilities to the world are

    _____

    _____

5. My responsibilities to God are

    _____

    _____

CHAPTER

1 Summary

Through careful reading of the above Torah passages from *Bereshit* you have gained a clearer understanding of the covenant between God and the Jewish people and how it was established. The Torah teaches that Abraham, as the first Jew, was the first person to believe in the one God. In the biblical world in which Abraham lived, most people believed that there were many gods, all of whom influenced certain limited aspects of the universe. Because Abraham rejected this dominant view and instead believed in one God, he was rewarded with a special promise we now know is called a *berit* ("covenant"). God repeated this *berit* to three generations of Jews through Abraham, Isaac, and Jacob. Each repetition of the *berit* underscores the promise that it will stand for all future generations of Jews.

SHEMOT/EXODUS:
The Song at the Sea and the Ten Commandments

About This Chapter: In this chapter you move on to the second book of the Torah, *Shemot*/Exodus. Apply the Torah study skills you gained in the last chapter to new excerpts from *Shemot*/Exodus. This book illustrates how the Israelites grow both physically, by increasing in numbers, and spiritually, by receiving the Torah and agreeing to obey its laws. As you read the Torah passages, focus on the progress of the Israelites from slavery to redemption to revelation.

66.74. From the collection of Hebrew Union College Skirball Museum

The Egyptians Being Drowned in the Red Sea. *Engraving, Germany, 17th century.*

Shemot/Exodus: From Slavery to Freedom

Shemot means "Names." Shemot begins by listing the names of Jacob's family members who accompanied him to Egypt. As you remember from *Bereshit*, Jacob is the third of the patriarchs to have received the *berit* from God. The last chapters of *Bereshit* describe how, despite the establishment of this covenant, Jacob's family, to escape famine, leaves the Promised Land and travels to Egypt. They settle in Egypt and grow into a large and prosperous community. But the good fortune of the Hebrew people* ends when a new pharaoh comes to power. He feels threatened by the multiplying numbers of Hebrews and decides to enslave them. The Hebrews come to experience miserable lives of backbreaking labor and cruelty.

*   During biblical times Jews were generally known as Hebrews, Israelites, or Judeans. The term Jew originally was given to the people living in Judea, the southern kingdom of the Land of Israel. After the destruction of the Temple in 586 B.C.E., the term Jew evolved into the name used for all followers of the Jewish religion.

27

Shemot tells not only of their gruelling life as slaves, but it also chronicles the miraculous rise of their leader, Moses. Moses, despite some early reservations, accepts the mission given to him by God and becomes the spokesperson for the Hebrew people. Moses leads the Israelites as they are redeemed from slavery and guides them through the awesome experience at Mount Sinai, where the scope of God's power is revealed and the Torah is received.

The Song at the Sea

Every year, at Pesach time, we read in the *haggadah* הַגָּדָה how God brings down ten plagues on the Egyptians to convince Pharaoh to let the Israelite slaves go. Finally, Pharaoh gives in and agrees to free the slaves. The slaves hurriedly pack and leave. In the meantime, Pharaoh changes his mind. Accompanied by his army, Pharaoh sets out in hot pursuit after the Israelites.

The fleeing Israelites soon reach the banks of a wide, deep body of water known as the Sea of Reeds or the Red Sea.[*] Suddenly, they turn and see Pharaoh and his men rapidly approaching. The Israelites are horrified. They are trapped between the sea and the advancing Egyptian army. Moses sees their fear and hesitation. He quickly turns to God for guidance and is told to lift up his rod and hold out his arm over the sea.

Miraculously the sea parts, and the Children of Israel cross the sea on dry ground. Just as the last of them crosses over to the other side, Pharaoh's men follow into the parted sea. At that instant the parted waters suddenly come together, and Pharaoh's men drown. Upon being saved, the Children of Israel spontaneously sing a joyous poem of thanksgiving and praise of God. This poem, known as *Shirat Hayam*, "Song at the Sea," is found in *Shemot* 15.

1] Then Moses and the Israelites sang this song to *Adonai.* They said: I will sing to *Adonai,* for God has triumphed gloriously;/ Horse and driver God has hurled into the sea./ **2]** *Adonai* is my strength and might;/ God is become my salvation./ This is my God and I will enshrine God;/ The God of my ancestors, and I will exalt God./ **3]** *Adonai,* the Warrior—/*Adonai* is God's name!/ **4]** Pharaoh's chariots and his army/God has cast into the sea;/ And the pick of his officers/ Are drowned in the Sea of Reeds./ **5]** The deeps covered them;/ They went down into the depths like a stone./ **6]** Your right hand, O *Adonai* glorious in power,/Your right

*The literal translation of the Hebrew Yam Suf יַם סוּף is the "Sea of Reeds." In later times this name was changed to the Red Sea.

28

hand, O *Adonai,* shatters the foe!/ **7]** In Your great triumph You break Your opponents;/ You send forth Your fury, it consumes them like straw./ **8]** At the blast of Your nostrils the waters piled up,/The floods stood straight like a wall;/The deeps froze in the heart of the sea./ **9]** The foe said,/"I will pursue, I will overtake,/I will divide the spoil;/My desire shall have its fill of them./ I will bare my sword—/My hand shall subdue them."/ **10]** You made Your wind blow, the sea covered them;/ They sank like lead in the majestic waters.

    11] Who is like You, O *Adonai,* among the celestials;/ Who is like You, majestic in holiness,/Awesome in splendor, working wonders!/ **12]** You put out Your right hand,/The earth swallowed them./ **13]** In Your love You lead the people You redeemed;/ In Your strength You guide them to Your holy abode./ **14]** The peoples hear, they tremble;/ Agony grips the dwellers in Philistia./ **15]** Now are the clans of Edom dismayed;/ The tribes of Moab—trembling grips them;/ All the dwellers in Canaan are aghast./ **16]** Terror and dread descend upon them;/ Through the might of Your arm they are still as stone—/Till Your people cross over, O *Adonai,*/Till Your people cross whom You have ransomed.

    17] You will bring them and plant them in Your own mountain,/The place You made to dwell in, O *Adonai,*/The sanctuary, O *Adonai,* which Your hands established./ **18]** *Adonai* will reign for ever and ever!

(Shemot 15:1-18)

ACTIVITIES

An anthropomorphism is a literary device used to describe something that is not human by using traits or characteristics normally used to describe human beings. In *Shirat Hayam* there are several anthropomorphisms. Locate at least one and explain it.

_____

_____

_____

The enthusiastic words praising God found in verses 11 and 18 are included in the *siddur* סִדּוּר ("prayer book") as part of the prayer *Mi Chamochah.* Using these verses as a model, write your own words of praise of God.

_____

_____

_____

29

The *Shirat Hayam, Shemot* 15, repeats, in poetry, the events described in prose in chapter 14. Why do you think this repetition is included in the Torah? Check off the answer(s) you like best.

1. To emphasize the joy of Moses and the Israelites upon being saved _____

2. To retell the events so they would not be forgotten _____

3. To give two different authors a chance to describe the events at the Sea of Reeds, one in prose and one in poetry _____

In the *haggadah* we read, "In every generation, every individual should feel personally redeemed from Egypt." We learn from this that we should all feel as if we were personally present at the events recorded in *Shemot*, including the going out of Egypt, the parting of the sea, and the receiving of the Torah. Write your own poem, song, or story describing what it was like when you were present at the parting of the sea.

_____

_____

_____

_____

_____

The Ten Commandments: Aseret Hadibrot

Soon after the miracle of the parting of the sea, we read in *Shemot* about another wondrous event. Amid lightning and thunder, Moses ascends Mount Sinai. A dense cloud surrounds the entire mountain. Down below, the Children of Israel anxiously wait for Moses to return with the words of the Torah from God. As the mountain trembles and the heavens shake, they witness the full extent of God's power. God speaks, and Moses records the words of the *Aseret Hadibrot*, "the Ten Commandments," found in *Shemot*.

1] God spoke all these words, saying:

2] I *Adonai* am your God who brought you out of the land of Egypt, the house of bondage: 3] You shall have no other gods beside Me.

4] You shall not make for yourself a sculptured image, or any likeness of what is in the heavens above, or on the earth below, or in the waters under the earth. **5]** You shall not bow down to them or serve them. For I *Adonai* your God am an impassioned God, visiting the guilt of the fathers upon the children, upon the third and upon the fourth generations of those who reject Me, **6]** but showing kindness to the thousandth generation of those who love Me and keep My commandments.

7] You shall not swear falsely by the name of *Adonai* your God; for *Adonai* will not clear one who swears falsely by God's name.

8] Remember the sabbath day and keep it holy. **9]** Six days you shall labor and do all your work, **10]** but the seventh day is a sabbath of *Adonai* your God: you shall not do any work—you, your son or daughter, your male or female slave, or your cattle, or the stranger who is within your settlements. **11]** For in six days *Adonai* made heaven and earth and sea, and all that is in them, and God rested on the seventh day; therefore *Adonai* blessed the sabbath day and hallowed it.

12] Honor your father and your mother, that you may long endure on the land which *Adonai* your God is giving you.

13] You shall not murder./ You shall not commit adultery./ You shall not steal./ You shall not bear false witness against your neighbor.

14] You shall not covet your neighbor's house: you shall not covet your neighbor's wife, or his male or female slave, or his ox or his ass, or anything that is your neighbor's.

(*Shemot* 20:1-14)☆

☆ *The Ten Commandments*

1. *I* Adonai *am your God...* *(verse 2)*

2. *You shall have no other gods beside Me.*
   You shall not make for yourself a sculptured image... (verses 3-6)

3. *You shall not swear falsely... (verse 7)*

4. *Remember the sabbath day... (verses 8-11)*

5. *Honor your father and your mother... (verse 12)*

6. *You shall not murder. (verse 13)*

7. *You shall not commit adultery. (verse 13)*

8. *You shall not steal. (verse 13)*

9. *You shall not bear false witness... (verse 13)*

10. *You shall not covet... (verse 14)*

God Speaks to Moses and the Israelites. *G. Hoet.*

The Torah commentator ibn Ezra wrote that the *mitzvot* can be divided into three categories: (1) commandments of the heart and mind (things we feel and think); (2) commandments of the mouth (things we say); and (3) commandments of doing (actions we take). Using these divisions, categorize the Ten Commandments.

Heart and Mind   Mouth   Doing

_____

One of the commandments requires that we honor our parents. If there were a commandment for parents to honor their children, how would it be worded?

_____

_____

The words of God as conveyed through Moses give us laws and rules to help us live as a community of Jews committed to God. Which of the Ten Commandments is the most important to you as a Jew? Why?

_____

_____

_____

The Ten Commandments also address matters of importance to all people. Which commandment is most important to you as a "citizen of the world"? Why?

_____

_____

_____

CHAPTER

2   Summary

At the foot of Mount Sinai we experience our true beginnings as a people. We arrived at Mount Sinai united through our common physical experiences of slavery, the Exodus from Egypt, and the crossing of the Sea of Reeds. When we received the Torah we were spiritually united through the *mitzvot* and teachings. Up until that moment, God had communicated only with individuals. In *Bereshit* we read how the *berit* was established through one-on-one encounters with Abraham, Isaac, and Jacob. At Mount Sinai, the moment God's power is revealed to the entire Jewish community, the *berit* becomes the possession of all Jews, from generation to generation.

VAYIKRA/LEVITICUS:
Sacrifices and the Holiness Code

About This Chapter: You now begin the study of the third book of the Torah, *Vayikra*/Leviticus. This book is different from *Bereshit* and *Shemot*. Instead of stories, it is filled mostly with descriptions of laws and rituals. Many of the rituals described in *Vayikra*/Leviticus are no longer practiced. One of your challenges, as you read this chapter, is to search for the meaning that these rituals still hold for us today.

Vayikra/Leviticus

Vayikra begins with the words "*Adonai* called to Moses and spoke to him . . . saying: Speak to the Israelite people, and say to them . . . ." God then describes to Moses the laws for offering sacrifices. Several chapters later, we find a description of the consecration of the priests and the dedication of the Tabernacle. *Vayikra* also contains a section on permitted and forbidden foods, which forms the basis for the laws of *kashrut*. The most often read and studied section of *Vayikra*/ Leviticus is found in chapter 19. This section, known as the Holiness Code, lists *mitzvot* that emphasize the idea that God wants us to be a holy people.

Sacrifices: An Ancient Form of Worship

Today when you want to pray with a community of other Jews you go to synagogue. You know that services will be held at certain times and on certain days. In ancient times, the Israelites, just like the religious groups who lived around them, brought sacrifices as their form of prayer. In most cases, the sacrifices of the Israelites consisted of food or drink. A portion was roasted and offered to God, and the rest was eaten by the sacrificer and his guests. The offering of these sacrifices followed a very specific structure and order. The details of these sacrifices are outlined in *Vayikra*. Some sacrifices were mandatory and performed at specific times. Other sacrifices were voluntary. In all cases, Aaron or his descendants, the priests, carried out the actual ritual of offering the sacrifices.＊

＊ *An Israelite was identified as a member of one of three groups:* Kohen כֹּהֵן *, a descendant of Aaron, responsible for preparing and offering all sacrifices;* Levi לֵוִי *, a descendant of Moses, responsible for assisting the priests (for example:* ritually washing the priests' hands*); or* Yisrael יִשְׂרָאֵל *, the remainder of the community. After the destruction of the Temple in 70 C.E., the group divisions remained in place to carry out certain rituals (for example:* the order in which people may be called up to the Torah for an *aliyah). Today only Orthodox and some Conservative communities continue paying attention to these divisions.*

The Tabernacle was the portable sanctuary that God commanded the Children of Israel to construct while they were in the desert. It was also known as the Tent of Meeting. It was believed that the Tabernacle was the abode of God. Therefore, all the sacrifices were offered in it, and the people felt protected by its presence.

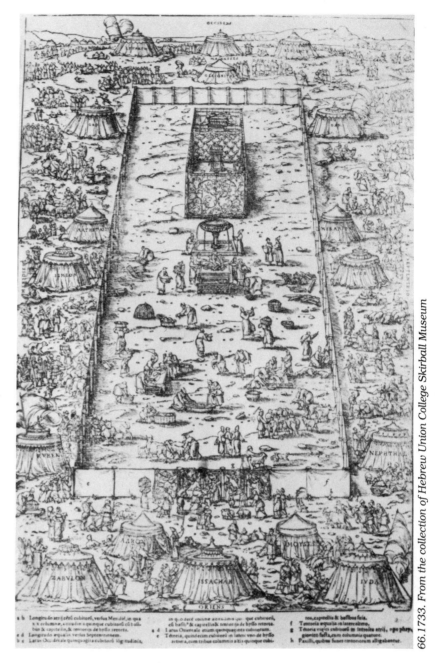

Atrium, Tabernaculum, Oblationes et Sacrificia Castra. *Engraving, Italy? 16th-17th centuries? After Benedictus Arias Montanus.*

The offering of sacrifices was the main way that Jews worshiped up until the destruction of the Second Temple in 70 C.E.

Various Vessels and Other Articles Used in the Temple of Solomon. *Engraving.*

Studying the detailed description of sacrifices in *Vayikra* helps us understand how ancient sacrifices and modern prayer are similar and dissimilar. Based on the information you have just read, fill in the chart below, which compares the two approaches to worship. Put a check if the item listed applies to sacrifices or prayer. (Some items will apply to both.)

	Sacrifices	Prayer
Can be an experience of the whole community		
Can be an experience of a single individual		
Is carried out according to a specific structure		
Is a way of asking forgiveness		
Is a form of giving thanks		
Requires a specially trained person to carry out		

The Law of Holiness

Chapter 19 of *Vayikra* teaches the importance of striving to live a good, holy life. The beginning of this chapter, "*Adonai* spoke to Moses, saying: Speak to the *whole* Israelite community and say to them," makes it clear that these *mitzvot* are for everybody to follow and not for just a select few. By following the *mitzvot*, we get closer to the goal of living a holy life. This same idea is expressed in many of our *berachot* ("blessings") when we recite the words *asher kideshanu bemitzvotav* ("who [God] makes us holy through the commandments").

While certain *mitzvot* in Chapter 19 might not touch on matters of concern for you today, the vast majority emphasizes the importance of holy behavior in every aspect of your day-to-day life. Even the *mitzvot* on sacrifices carry a message for today. They emphasize that worship in any form must be undertaken with a careful and sincere approach. This chapter of the Torah offers a combination of moral as well as ceremonial commandments, all aimed at helping us live lives of holiness.

1] *Adonai* spoke to Moses, saying: **2]** Speak to the whole Israelite community and say to them:

You shall be holy, for I, *Adonai* your God, am holy.

3] You shall each revere your mother and father, and keep My sabbaths: I *Adonai* am your God.

4] Do not turn to idols or make molten gods for yourselves: I *Adonai* am your God.

5] When you sacrifice an offering of well-being to *Adonai,* sacrifice it so that it may be accepted on your behalf. **6]** It shall be eaten on the day you sacrifice it, or on the day following; but what is left by the third day must be consumed in fire. **7]** If it should be eaten on the third day, it is an offensive thing, it will not be acceptable. **8]** And he who eats of it shall bear his guilt, for he has profaned what is sacred to *Adonai;* that person shall be cut off from his kin.

9] When you reap the harvest of your land, you shall not reap all the way to the edges of your field, or gather the gleanings of your harvest. **10]** You shall not pick your vineyard bare, or gather the fallen fruit of your vineyard; you shall leave them for the poor and the stranger: I *Adonai* am your God.

11] You shall not steal; you shall not deal deceitfully or falsely with one another. **12]** You shall not swear falsely by My name, profaning the name of your God: I am *Adonai.*

13] You shall not defraud your neighbor. You shall not commit robbery. The wages of a laborer shall not remain with you until morning.

14] You shall not insult the deaf, or place a stumbling block before the blind. You shall fear your God: I am *Adonai.*

15] You shall not render an unfair decision: do not favor the poor or show deference to the rich; judge your neighbor fairly. **16]** Do not deal basely with your fellows. Do not profit by the blood of your neighbor: I am *Adonai.*

17] You shall not hate your kinsfolk in your heart. Reprove your neighbor, but incur no guilt because of him. **18]** You shall not take vengeance or bear a grudge against your kinsfolk. Love your neighbor as yourself: I am *Adonai.*

(*Vayikra* 19:1-18)

As you read the Holiness Code you probably noticed many similarities with the Ten Commandments. Complete the comparison chart below.

	Holiness Code (use the verse number)
Ten Commandments	
1. I *Adonai* am your God.	_____
2. You shall have no other gods.	_____
3. You shall not swear falsely.	_____
4. Remember the Sabbath day.	_____
5. Honor your father and your mother.	_____
6. You shall not murder.	_____
7. You shall not commit adultery.	_____
8. You shall not steal.	_____
9. You shall not bear false witness.	_____
10. You shall not covet.	_____

The message of the Holiness Code is that a holy people is created not just through performing ceremonial acts but also through the actions of everyday life. Verses 9-18 include normal everyday activities, like farming and doing business, and relations between community members. Find and write out one example of each.

A *mitzvah* that mentions farming: _____

_____

A *mitzvah* that mentions business affairs: _____

_____

A *mitzvah* that mentions relations between community members:

_____

Based on all you have learned, how would you define living a holy life? Write a definition that you could really try to live by. _____

_____

_____

The *mitzvah* known as the Golden Rule appears in *Vayikra* 19:18. Rabbi Akiva, about whom you read in the Introduction, thought that "Love your neighbor as yourself" was one of the greatest *mitzvot* of the Torah. Write a real-life example or create a story that illustrates this *mitzvah*. _____

_____

_____

_____

_____

CHAPTER

3 Summary

Through Torah study you learn about the rich history of the Jewish people. You also are challenged to find meaning for today from descriptions of the rituals and practices of the past. *Vayikra* offers you many lessons for living today. The chapters on sacrifices and appropriate priestly behavior teach that worship, no matter what the form, must be done with sincerity and respect.

Vayikra also teaches that the path to a holy life is achieved not only through prayer but also through your actions towards your fellow human beings. And *Vayikra* gives you a very simple guideline to follow. When deciding how to act towards another person, be guided by the ideal to treat others in the same way that you hope they will treat you.

BEMIDBAR/NUMBERS:
Spies and Rebels

CHAPTER 4

About This Chapter: *Bemidbar*/Numbers is the fourth book of the Torah. *Bemidbar*/Numbers takes you back to the desert and to the wanderings of the Children of Israel. In this chapter you will encounter stories that display the honesty of some and the lies of others. You will read also about the difficulty of keeping the people unified under the harsh conditions of the desert. And finally you will explore how the rebelliousness of a few can challenge the courage of the whole community.

Bemidbar/Numbers

Shemot ends with the building of the Tabernacle. *Vayikra* takes a break in the action and focuses on teaching us laws for living a holy life according to the *mitzvot*. With *Bemidbar* we return to where we left off with *Shemot*. Once again we find ourselves wandering in the desert with the Children of Israel. The time is approximately one year after the Exodus from Egypt and one month after the completion of the Tabernacle.

Bemidbar begins with a census. A section covering many legal topics follows. Next, we read of the consecration of the Tabernacle. Then we turn to the wanderings of the Children of Israel in the wilderness and the adventure of the spies, who are sent to check out things in the future homeland.

The Return of the Spies. *R. Seinweber, illustration.*

The Spies

The time for the Children of Israel to enter the Promised Land is fast approaching. But they cannot just claim the land without a military struggle. So God tells Moses to choose twelve representatives, one from each tribe, to scout Canaan. Moses gives them very specific instructions about what they are to look for. They are then to report back.

1] *Adonai* spoke to Moses, saying, 2] "Send men to scout the land of Canaan, which I am giving to the Israelite people; send one man from each of their ancestral tribes, each one a chieftain among them." 3] So Moses, by *Adonai's* command, sent them out from the wilderness of Paran, all the men being leaders of the Israelites.

(*Bemidbar* 13:1-3)

17] When Moses sent them to scout the land of Canaan, he said to them, "Go up there into the Negeb and on into the hill country, 18] and see what kind of country it is. Are the people who dwell in it strong or weak, few or many? 19] Is the country in which they dwell good or bad? Are the towns they live in open or fortified? 20] Is the soil rich or poor? Is it wooded or not? And take pains to bring back some of the fruit of the land." — Now it happened to be the season of the first ripe grapes.

21] They went up and scouted the land. . . . 23] They reached the wadi Eshcol, and there they cut down a branch with a single cluster of grapes—it had to be borne on a carrying frame by two of them—and some pomegranates and figs....

25] At the end of forty days they returned from scouting the land. 26] They went straight to Moses and Aaron and the whole Israelite community at Kadesh in the wilderness of Paran, and they made their report to them and to the whole community, as they showed them the fruit of the land. 27] This is what they told him: "We came to the land you sent us to; it does indeed flow with milk and honey, and this is its fruit. 28] However, the people who inhabit the country are powerful, and the cities are fortified and very large; moreover, we saw the Anakites there....

30] Caleb hushed the people before Moses and said, "Let us by all means go up, and we shall gain possession of it, for we shall surely overcome it."

31] But the men who had gone up with him said, "We cannot attack that people, for it is stronger than we." **32]** Thus they spread calumnies among the Israelites about the land they had scouted, saying, "The country that we traversed and scouted is one that devours its settlers. All the people that we saw in it are men of great size; **33]** we saw the Nephilim there – the Anakites are part of the Nephilim – and we looked like grasshoppers to ourselves, and so we must have looked to them."

(*Bemidbar* 13:17-33)

1] The whole community broke into loud cries, and the people wept that night. **2]** All the Israelites railed against Moses and Aaron. "If only we had died in the land of Egypt," the whole community shouted at them, "or if only we might die in this wilderness! **3]** Why is *Adonai* taking us to that land to fall by the sword? Our wives and children will be carried off! It would be better for us to go back to Egypt!" **4]** And they said to one another, "Let us head back for Egypt."

5] Then Moses and Aaron fell on their faces before all the assembled congregation of the Israelites. **6]** And Joshua son of Nun and Caleb son of Jephunneh, of those who had scouted the land, rent their clothes* **7]** and exhorted the whole Israelite community: "The land that we traversed and scouted is an exceedingly good land. **8]** If *Adonai* is pleased with us, God will bring us into that land, a land that flows with milk and honey, and give it to us; **9]** only you must not rebel against *Adonai*. Have no fear then of the people of the country, for they are our prey: their protection has departed from them, but *Adonai* is with us. Have no fear of them!" **10]** As the whole community threatened to pelt them with stones, the Presence of *Adonai* appeared in the Tent of the Meeting to all the Israelites.

(*Bemidbar* 14:1-10)

* *When Joshua and Caleb heard the commotion in the community over the false reports of the spies, they tore their clothes. This is a sign of mourning. What do you think Joshua and Caleb were mourning? The death of the possibility of entering the land? The future death of the spies who had lied? The depth of their sadness over the false reports?*

God becomes very frustrated by the Israelites' lack of faith and courage. After much discussion between God and Moses, God punishes all the spies with death by plague – that is, all the spies except for Caleb and Joshua. They, of course, were the only ones who did not spread lies about the Promised Land and had faith that God would lead them to victory in conquering the enemies of the land.

What is the significance of each item Moses told the spies to check out? Match the items on the left with the appropriate answer on the right.

A. the size of the population   ____ 1. how good the land is for agriculture

B. the existence of walls around the towns   ____ 2. strong people are harder to defeat

C. the quality of the soil   ____ 3. a large population can mean bigger opposing armies

D. the strength of the people   ____ 4. expectations of future food supplies

E. the quality of the fruits   ____ 5. walled cities are more difficult to attack

How do you explain the fact that Joshua and Caleb had one view of what they saw in Canaan and the ten other spies had a very different view? Which of the following expresses your opinion of the best answer to this question?

____ 1. The ten spies who gave the negative report did not purposely lie about what they saw; rather, they lacked the courage to face the task of conquering the land. Therefore, they did not focus on the positive things.

____ 2. The fear expressed by the ten spies was a very human reaction to what they had seen.

____ 3. Joshua and Caleb saw the same frightening things, but they gave a more positive report because they had faith that God would help them conquer the land.

4. Other

_____

_____

_____

Describe an experience from your life that you shared with someone else that resulted in different reports as to what had happened. (*Example:* A fight with your brother or sister; an accident; an encounter with the school bully.)

_____

_____

_____

43

Gustave Doré, France, 1865

Korah, Dathan, and Abiram.

Discontentment among the People: Korah, Dathan, and Abiram

* *The Torah tells us that God provided the Children of Israel with food that fell from the sky each day. (A double portion fell on Friday since it could not be collected on Shabbat.) It was called manna. One midrash states that manna tasted like whatever the person eating it wanted it to taste like. Like what food would your manna have tasted?*

Following the episode with the spies, more turmoil hits the community. The harsh life in the desert begins to take its toll on the Children of Israel. The days are brutally hot. The nights uncomfortably cold. Their next source of water is uncertain. Their food, while plentiful, is rather weird. It falls from heaven for them to collect each day.* The Children of Israel wonder if they were not better off back in Egypt. Sure they had to work hard. But there was certainty and regularity to their days. They woke up each morning and knew what to expect. In the desert the only certainty is sand. They do not know what tomorrow will bring. They are losing faith in their leadership. In *Bemidbar* 16 you will discover how three men, Korah, Dathan, and Abiram, respond to this situation.

1] Now Korah, son of Izhar son of Kohath son of Levi, betook himself, along with Dathan and Abiram sons of Eliab, and On son of Peleth—descendants of Reuben— **2]** to rise up against Moses, together with two hundred and fifty Israelites, chieftains of the community, chosen in the assembly, men of repute. **3]** They combined against Moses and Aaron and said to them, "You have gone too far! For all the community are holy, all of them, and *Adonai* is in their midst. Why then do you raise yourselves above *Adonai's* congregation?"

4] When Moses heard this, he fell on his face. **5]** Then he spoke to Korah and all his company, saying, "Come morning, *Adonai* will make known who is God and who is holy, and will grant that person access to God; God will grant access to the one God has chosen. **6]** Do this: You, Korah and all your band, take fire pans, **7]** and tomorrow put fire in them and lay incense on them before *Adonai.* Then the man whom *Adonai* chooses, he shall be the holy one. You have gone too far, sons of Levi!"

(Bemidbar 16:1-7)

At the same time that Moses confronts Korah and his band, he must also try to deal directly with Dathan and Abiram. However, they do not come when Moses calls.

12] Moses sent for Dathan and Abiram, sons of Eliab; but they said, "We will not come! **13]** Is it not enough that you brought us from a land flowing with milk and honey to have us die in the wilderness, that you would also lord it over us? **14]** Even if you had brought us to a land flowing with milk and honey, and given us possession of fields and vineyards, should you gouge out those men's eyes? We will not come!" **15]** Moses was much aggrieved and he said to *Adonai,* "Pay no regard to their oblation [sacrifice]. I have not taken the ass of any one of them, nor have I wronged any one of them."

(Bemidbar 16:12-15)

ACTIVITIES

According to Moses, how will this dispute over the leadership be decided? Who will determine who are the true leaders? _____

_____

_____

True or False. Based on your reading of this excerpt from *Bemidbar* 16:12-15, write True or False next to these statements.

_____   Dathan and Abiram refused to appear at Moses' request because they resented being in the wilderness where he had brought them.

_____   Dathan and Abiram felt Moses had misled them.

_____   Moses told God to ignore the sacrifices of Dathan and Abiram and assured God that the complaints of the rebels had no basis in fact.

What are the specific complaints that the people have against Moses? Prepare a petition, listing their complaints, that the rebels would have been willing to sign.

We the undersigned list the following complaints about our leader Moses:

_____

_____

_____

_____

Finally the day of the test to prove the true leadership arrives. The air fills with tension. Korah and his followers prepare their offerings to God in their fire pans. Moses and Aaron do the same. The entire community crowds round. Some support the rebellion of Korah; others are there merely to watch the drama unfold. Upon seeing the large gathering, God is angered and threatens to destroy the entire community. *Adonai* speaks to Moses and Aaron saying, "Stand back from this community that I may annihilate them in an instant!" But Moses and Aaron are distraught and cry out, "O God, Source of the breath of all flesh! When one person sins, will You be wrathful with the whole community?" God responds to their pleas by withdrawing the threat. Instead God directs Moses to tell the community to stand back and separate themselves from the rebels and their followers. The moment of truth arrives.

27] ...Now Dathan and Abiram had come out and they stood at the entrance of their tents, with their wives, their children, and their little ones. 28] And Moses said, "By this you shall know that it was *Adonai* who sent me to do all these things; that they are not of my own devising: **29]** if these men die as all men do, if their lot be the common fate of all humanity, it was not *Adonai* who sent me. **30]** But if *Adonai* brings about something unheard-of, so that the ground opens its mouth wide and swallows them up with all that belongs to them, and they go down alive into Sheol, you shall know that these men have spurned *Adonai*." **31]** Scarcely had he finished speaking all these words when the ground under them burst asunder, **32]** and the earth opened its mouth and swallowed them up with their households, all Korah's people and all their possessions. **33]** They went down alive into Sheol, with all that belonged to them; the earth closed over them and they vanished from the midst of the congregation. **34]** All Israel around them fled at their shrieks, for they said, "The earth might swallow us!"

35] And a fire went forth from *Adonai* and consumed the two hundred and fifty men offering the incense.

(*Bemidbar* 16:27-35)

ACTIVITY

The rebels succeeded in making known their complaints. In the end all they accomplished was to anger God, Moses, and Aaron. Do some methods of protest work better than others? _____ Suggest alternative approaches Korah, Dathan, and Abiram could have tried to get their points across. Include ideas for a peaceful settlement of this situation. _____

_____

_____

_____

CHAPTER

4 **Summary**

Bemidbar shares with us more of the desert experiences of the Children of Israel. We read of the fear stirred up by the false reports of the spies. From Caleb and Joshua we are reminded of the importance of the truth and having the courage to keep our faith in God. We see how the disastrous results of the rebellion of Korah, Dathan, and Abiram worked to fuel the flames of uneasiness and doubt in the community.

Bemidbar emphasizes the uncertainties and difficulties of life in the desert. But it also focuses attention on the need for the Children of Israel to remember the God who "brought them out of the house of Egypt" and to hold on to their faith that God will protect them in the desert and bring them safely to the Promised Land.

Moses. *Michelangelo Buonarroti, sculpture, 1545.*

DEVARIM/DEUTERONOMY:
Moses' Last Speech

About This Chapter: *Devarim*/Deuteronomy is the fifth and final book of the Torah. In this book the wandering of the Jewish people comes to an end and so does the life of their leader, Moses. As you read the Torah passages, consider the impact that Moses' life had on the Children of Israel. Also focus on the major themes that Moses emphasizes in his farewell speech.

Devarim/Deuteronomy

In *Devarim*/Deuteronomy Moses summarizes, reviews, and repeats the key laws found in the first four books of the Torah. The theme of *berit* ("covenant") first mentioned in *Bereshit* runs through all the books of the Torah. In *Devarim*/Deuteronomy, Moses reminds the Children of Israel that their part in the *berit* obligates them to follow the laws set down by God. The Children of Israel stand east of the Jordan River on the doorstep of the Promised Land* and listen carefully as Moses reviews their forty years of wandering, restating the instructions, laws, warnings, blessings, and curses found in the first four books of the Torah.

He also describes an inviting picture of the Promised Land. Near the end of *Devarim*/Deuteronomy Moses bids farewell in a moving speech. Then the closing chapters tell of Moses' last days: his preparations for death, his choice of Joshua as his successor, and his parting instructions to Joshua and the priests. *Devarim*/Deuteronomy concludes on a solemn note with the death of Moses.

* The homeland of the Jews has had many names throughout our history. When God established the berit with Abraham, the land he promised him was called Canaan. During the time of the Second Temple it came to be known as Judea. After the destruction of the Second Temple (70 C.E.), in rabbinic literature, it was called Eretz Yisrael, "the Land of Israel," or the shortened form Ha'aretz, "the Land." Roman Emperor Hadrian (76-138 C.E.) gave it the name Syria Palestine. In time, it became known simply as Palestine, which was used until 1948 when the modern State of Israel was established.

Moses Gives a Farewell Speech

Moses, the greatest leader in Jewish history, is first mentioned in *Shemot*. He becomes God's spokesperson and pleads for the slaves to be freed. When Pharaoh finally agrees, Moses leads the Children of Israel out of Egypt and into the desert. Throughout all the forty years of wandering in the wilderness, Moses serves as the leader of the Jewish nation. He works hard in his role as an intermediary between God and the Israelites. He begs God to forgive the Israelites when they stray from the law; he urges the Children of Israel to do as

God commands and requires. Sometimes Moses gets angry and frustrated, but he never gives up. Even when he is personally denied the privilege of entering the Promised Land, the Land of Israel, he maintains his leadership role.

As Moses stands at the border, he reminds the Israelites of all they must do to uphold the *berit* with God. The children of Israel listen with great attention as Moses begins his farewell address.

9] You stand this day, all of you, before *Adonai* your God— your tribal heads, your elders and your officials, all the men of Israel, **10]** your children, your wives, even the stranger within your camp, from woodchopper to waterdrawer—**11]** to enter into the covenant of *Adonai* your God, which *Adonai* your God is concluding with you this day, with its sanctions; **12]** to the end that God may establish you this day as God's people and be your God, as God promised you and as God swore to your fathers, Abraham, Isaac, and Jacob. **13]** I make this covenant, with its sanctions, not with you alone, **14]** but both with those who are standing here with us this day before *Adonai* our God and with those who are not with us here this day.

(Devarim 29:9-14)

11] Surely, this Instruction which I enjoin upon you this day is not too baffling for you, nor is it beyond reach. **12]** It is not in the heavens, that you should say, "Who among us can go up to the heavens and get it for us and impart it to us, that we may observe it?" **13]** Neither is it beyond the sea, that you should say, "Who among us can cross to the other side of the sea and get it for us and impart it to us, that we may observe it?" **14]** No, the thing is very close to you, in your mouth and in your heart, to observe it.

(Devarim 30:11-14)

📖 **ACTIVITIES**

What words in *Devarim* 29:9-14 underscore the idea that God intends for the *berit* to be with all Jews throughout history? Reread *Devarim* 29:9-14 and underline the key phrases that emphasize this idea.

Write a play using *Devarim* 30:11-14. Moses' lines are already supplied. Fill in the lines of the Israelites.

Isralites: _____

_____

Moses: Surely, this Instruction which I enjoin upon you this day is not too baffling for you, nor is it beyond reach.

Israelites: _____

_____

Moses: It is not in the heavens, that you should say, "Who among us can go up to the heavens and get it for us and impart it to us, that we may observe it?"

Israelites: _____

_____

Moses: Neither is it beyond the sea, that you should say, "Who among us can cross to the other side of the sea and get it for us and impart it to us, that we may observe it?"

Israelites: _____

_____

Moses: No, the thing is very close to you, in your mouth and in your heart, to observe it.

The Death of Moses

The last chapter of *Devarim*/Deuteronomy, the last of the Five Books of Moses, reports the death of the Jewish people's greatest leader.

5] So Moses the servant of *Adonai* died there, in the land of Moab, at the command of the Eternal. 6] God buried him in the valley in the land of Moab, near Beth-peor; and no one knows his burial place to this day.* 7] Moses was a hundred and twenty years old when he died; his eyes were undimmed and his vigor unabated. 8] And the Israelites bewailed Moses in the steppes of Moab for thirty days.

* The Torah tells us that the burial place of Moses is unknown. Why do you think it is unknown? If it were known, what do you think might have happened there?

51

Moses and the Burning Bush.

Lynd Ward, illustration

The period of wailing and mourning for Moses came to an end. **9]** Now Joshua son of Nun was filled with the spirit of wisdom because Moses had laid his hands upon him; and the Israelites heeded him, doing as *Adonai* had commanded Moses.

10] Never again did there arise in Israel a prophet like Moses—whom *Adonai* singled out, face to face, **11]** for the various signs and portents that *Adonai* sent him to display in the land of Egypt, against Pharaoh and all his courtiers and his whole country, **12]** and for all the great might and awesome power that Moses displayed before all Israel.

(*Devarim* 34:5-12)

God says to Moses, "This is the land of which I swore to Abraham, Isaac, and Jacob, 'I will give it to your offspring.' I have let you see it with your own eyes, but you shall not cross there." (34:4) Assume the role of Moses. Write a letter to God before you die. Are you satisfied with your life? Are you ready to die? Are you content to have seen but not entered the Promised Land?

Dear God,

_____

_____

_____

Your humble servant,
Moses

Who wrote the verses about the death of Moses? One traditional opinion is that Moses wrote the whole Torah, including the last chapter reporting his own death. According to another opinion, Moses' successor, Joshua, wrote *Devarim* 34:5-12. This second view raises another question. How could Joshua write of the death and burial of Moses when the Torah tell us "no one knows his burial place to this day"? Write your explanation of who wrote the verses and how.

_____

_____

_____

CHAPTER

5   Summary

This chapter concludes your study of the Five Books of Moses. You have tasted only a small portion of the total contents with just a few of its passages. Nonetheless, you have moved from the beginnings of the Jewish people to their arrival in the Land of Israel. You know that the *berit* established in *Bereshit* is a common thread that connects all the books of the Torah, and you understand that the Israelites' entrance into the Promised Land represented an important step toward the fulfillment of God's *berit* with the Jewish people.

Devarim ends with the death of Moses and the end of an era. In coming chapters we will learn more of the Israelites' struggle to become a nation and settle the Land of Israel.

Prophets and Writings

About This Unit: The Jewish Bible consists of more than the Torah, the Five Books of Moses. But what exactly are the other parts of the Bible, and what are their contents? How and when was the Jewish Bible finally organized? What qualified a book to be included in the Jewish Bible? These are just some of the questions you will explore in this section.

Megillat Esther. *Parchment, Balkan, pre-1700.*

The Book of Esther is one of the books included in the Ketuvim, the Writings, the third section of the Tanach.

Tanach: What's in a Name?

Did you know that one of the names used for the Jewish Bible is an acronym? An acronym is a word created by combining the initial letters of several words. The Jewish Bible consists of three parts: *Torah*, the Five Books of Moses; *Nevi'im*, the Prophets; and *Ketuvim*, the Writings. When you take the first letters of the three section names and add a few vowels you get **TaNaCH**. *Tanach* is the name used by many Jews for the whole Jewish Bible. By now you are familiar with the first part of the *Tanach*, the Torah. You know that it includes five books, *Bereshit*, *Shemot*, *Vayikra*, *Bemidbar*, and *Devarim*. But what about the other two sections, *Nevi'im* and *Ketuvim*? To find out what is included in the second and third parts of the *Tanach*, read on.

Hosea the Prophet. *"The Assyrians in Samaria," circa 800s B.C. From a series of the prophets, Dutch engravings, 16th century.*

Nevi'im/Prophets

The second section of the *Tanach* is *Nevi'im* ("Prophets"). The term prophet means spokesperson. The prophets received the word of God and served as spokepersons by delivering God's messages to the people. In *Nevi'im*, the record of the Children of Israel's story continues where *Devarim* leaves off. The narrative historical books—Joshua, Judges, I Samuel and II Samuel, and I Kings and II Kings—describe how the Children of Israel conquer and settle the new land and how they develop as a community. These books are called the "Former Prophets." The rest of *Nevi'im* consists of a series of more poetic books labeled the "Latter Prophets." The "Latter Prophets" are further divided into two groups. The first group of the "Latter Prophets" includes Isaiah, Jeremiah, and Ezekiel. The second group, known as the "Twelve Minor Prophets," includes Hosea, Joel, Amos, Obadiah, Jonah, Micah, Nahum, Habakkuk, Zephaniah, Haggai, Zechariah, and Malachi. These books are not called "minor" because they are unimportant, but rather because they are relatively short in length. Each of the books of *Nevi'im* gets its title from the central figure in the book or from the name of the person who is supposed to have written the book. (We say "supposed to have written" because in some cases the author is not known for certain.) The chart below shows the divisions of the books of *Nevi'im*.

Former Prophets	Latter Prophets	
Joshua	Isaiah	Hosea
Judges	Jeremiah	Joel
I Samuel	Ezekiel	Amos
II Samuel	The Twelve	Obadiah
I Kings	"Minor" Prophets	Jonah
II Kings		Micah
		Nahum
		Habakkuk
		Zephaniah
		Haggai
		Zechariah
		Malachi

Ketuvim/Writings

The third part of the *Tanach, Ketuvim*/Writings, includes a wide-ranging collection of books. Some books are poetic: Psalms, Song of Songs, and Lamentations. Then there are the books known as wisdom literature, which tend to be philosophical—Proverbs, Job, and Ecclesiastes. The story of the Jewish people continues to be told in the historical books: Ruth, Esther, Ezra, Nehemiah, and Chronicles I and II. And, finally, in a class all of its own, is the blend of history and prophecy known as the Book of Daniel. The books in *Ketuvim* are ordered as follows: Psalms, Proverbs, Job, Song of Songs, Ruth, Lamentations, Ecclesiastes, Esther, Daniel, Ezra, Nehemiah, I Chronicles, and II Chronicles.

Canonization: What's In and What's Out?

Now that all the books of the *Tanach* have been introduced, we move on to the question of how it was decided which would be included and which would not. As you might guess, the answer to this question is not simple.

The term canonize describes the process of making final decisions about which books would be included in the Jewish Bible. We do not know exactly when or by whom each of the three sections of the *Tanach* was canonized. We do know that the *Tanach* represents the final selection process that covered many centuries. ☆ The decision to include some of the books—particularly the five books of the Torah—may have been made as early as 400 B.C.E. The final form of *Nevi'im* was established when it was canonized around 200 B.C.E. And the ultimate formation of *Ketuvim*, the third and final section of the *Tanach*, occurred several hundred years later, sometime around 100-200 C.E.

Even with the establishment of these dates the question remains: How was what was in and what was out decided? The most direct answer to this question is that any book considered to be either revealed by God or inspired by God was included in the *Tanach*. The books that qualified are considered sacred. They include books of beautiful literary style; books of important Jewish rituals; and books that focus on the growth of the nation and appeal to the national pride of the people.

☆ *What Is the Apocrypha?*

When the Tanach *was completed and all the choices made about what was in and what was out, there were many books that had been considered and rejected. This collection of books, known as the Apocrypha, includes some familiar books like I Maccabees and II Maccabees and the book of Judith, which are associated with the holiday of Chanukah. The books of the Apocrypha follow the main style and form of the books of the* Tanach. *But, because they were not included in the* Tanach, *we do not consider them sacred texts.*

Unit Two: Summary

The entire *Tanach* is too vast to study in detail at this time. But at least you now have an idea of the makeup and structure of the three parts of the Jewish Bible. Now it is time to move on to the next chapter where you will examine a few excerpts from the second part of the *Tanach, Nevi'im.*

NEVI'IM/PROPHETS:
The Rise of the Monarchy

About This Chapter: A new era in the history of the Jewish people begins in I Samuel and II Samuel, the third and fourth books of *Nevi'im*. In these books the first Jewish kings are anointed. This development raises many questions that you should consider as you read this chapter: How can a people who are governed by God, the Supreme Ruler, also be ruled by a human king? What qualities best suit a person to serve as king? When a king makes mistakes, how does God react?

M.638, f.25. Courtesy of the Pierpont Morgan Library, New York

The Prophet Samuel Selects David, the Shepherd, to Be King.

I Samuel and II Samuel

For centuries, since the time of Abraham, the Jewish people lived under the rule of God. God appointed such leaders as Abraham, Isaac, Jacob, Moses, Joshua, and Deborah. These leaders served as prophets or spokespersons of God. They guided the Jewish people according to the instructions they received from God. In the books of I Samuel and II Samuel we read that the Children of Israel are no longer satisfied with this system of leadership. They decide they want to follow the model of the nations around them and be ruled by a human king. I Samuel and II Samuel describe the rise of the monarchy of the Jewish nation. The titles of these books come from the prophet Samuel, the first major personality to be mentioned in them.

Samuel serves as a prophet and the leader of Israel

until his old age when he appoints his sons to take over for him. However, the Israelites complain that Samuel's sons are not following in his footsteps. They ask Samuel to appoint someone as king to rule over them. So Samuel prays to God for guidance and does as God instructs him. He anoints the man to whom God guides him, Saul, as the first king of the Jewish people.☆ Saul is not a successful king and God sends Samuel to find another. The following excerpts from I Samuel tell about Samuel's search for a new king.

1] And *Adonai* said to Samuel, "How long will you grieve over Saul, since I have rejected him as king over Israel? Fill your horn with oil and set out; I am sending you to Jesse the Bethlehemite, for I have decided on one of his sons to be king." 2] Samuel replied, "How can I go? If Saul hears of it, he will kill me." *Adonai* answered, "Take a heifer with you, and say, 'I have come to sacrifice to *Adonai*.' 3] Invite Jesse to the sacrificial feast, and then I will make known to you what you shall do; you shall anoint for Me the one I point out to you." 4] Samuel did what *Adonai* commanded. When he came to Bethlehem, the elders of the city went out in alarm to meet him and said, "Do you come on a peaceful errand?" 5] "Yes," he replied, "I have come to sacrifice to *Adonai*. Purify yourselves and join me in the sacrificial feast." He also instructed Jesse and his sons to purify themselves and invited them to the sacrificial feast.☆

6] When they arrived and he saw Eliab, he thought: "Surely *Adonai*'s anointed stands before God." 7] But *Adonai* said to Samuel, "Pay no attention to his appearance or his stature, for I have rejected him. For not as people see [does *Adonai* see]; people see only what is visible, but the Eternal sees into the heart." 8] Then Jesse called Abinadab and had him pass before Samuel; but he said, "*Adonai* has not chosen this one either." 9] Next Jesse presented Shammah; and again he said, "The Eternal has not chosen this one either." 10] Thus Jesse presented seven of his sons before Samuel, and Samuel said to Jesse, "*Adonai* has not chosen any of these."

11] Then Samuel asked Jesse, "Are these all the boys you have?" He replied, "There is still the youngest; he is tending the flock." And Samuel said to Jesse, "Send someone to bring him, for we will not sit down to eat until he gets here." 12] So they sent and brought him. He was ruddy-cheeked, bright-eyed, and handsome. And *Adonai* said, "Rise and anoint him, for this is the one." 13] Samuel took the horn of oil and anointed him in the presence of his brothers; and the spirit of *Adonai* gripped David from that day on. Samuel then set out for Ramah.

(*I Samuel* 16:1-13)

☆ In ancient Israel a king was anointed with oil as a sign of his taking on this important position. Oil was poured from a horn onto his head. The act of anointing a king signified that he was supported by the strength and wisdom of God.

☆ In ancient times sacrifices were a form of praying to God. Before anyone could participate in the offering of a sacrifice, they had to purify themselves by bathing in a special ritual bath.

ACTIVITIES

Below are several ideas expressed in I Samuel 16:1-13. Match the idea on the left with the correct verse number on the right.

    A.   Samuel must not dwell on the   _____ 1. 16:13
          failure of Saul but move on.

    B.   God can judge a person   _____ 2. 16:1
          better than another person can.

    C.   God, not Samuel, appoints   _____ 3. 16:7
          David to be king.

What do we know about David after reading the above verses? Check as many as are correct.

    _____ 1. David is a handsome young man.

    _____ 2. David is a shepherd.

    _____ 3. God, not Samuel, picked David.

    _____ 4. David has great leadership qualities.

This text from I Samuel does not tell us how David's brothers reacted to being passed over in favor of their youngest brother. Which of the statements below do you think might describe their feelings? Why?

    _____ 1. They are jealous and angry.

    _____ 2. They are excited that their youngest brother has been chosen because they think that as brothers of the future king they will get special privileges.

    _____ 3. They are proud of him.

    _____ 4. Since the text does not say how they feel, they probably did not care one way or the other.

Make a list of at least five traits that you think are important for a good leader of government such as a king, president, or prime minister.

    _____   _____   _____   _____   _____

David Dances before the Ark.

David as King

David does not assume the kingship as soon as Samuel anoints him. First he serves as a loyal servant to Saul. He plays the harp to calm Saul's nerves and fights in the army against Saul's enemies. David amazes everyone with his astounding victory over Goliath. The heroic feat wins him a promotion to captain and the honor of marrying Saul's daughter, Michal. David also forms a deep friendship with Jonathan, the son of Saul. But, instead of rejoicing in David's successes and in his growing ties to his family, Saul grows more and more jealous and suspicious of David. Frightened by Saul's rage against him, David flees the royal court.

He escapes Saul's army by traveling around the country and gathering together his own army of supporters. When Saul dies in battle against the Philistines, David finally begins his reign as king.

During his forty-year reign, David accomplishes a great deal towards the goal of unifying the tribes of Israel both politically and spiritually. He captures Jerusalem and makes it Israel's political capital. But even more importantly he makes Jerusalem the nation's religious center. To learn how he accomplishes this, read the following verses from II Samuel.

12] It was reported to King David: *"Adonai* has blessed Obed-edom's house and all that belongs to him because of the Ark of God." Thereupon David went and brought up the Ark of God from the house of Obed-edom to the City of David, amid rejoicing. **13]** When the bearers of the Ark of *Adonai* had moved forward six paces, he sacrificed an ox and a fatling. **14]** David whirled with all his might before *Adonai*; David was girt with a linen *ephod.* **15]** Thus David and all the House of Israel brought up the Ark of *Adonai* with shouts and with blasts of the horn.

16] As the Ark of *Adonai* entered the City of David, Michal daughter of Saul looked out of the window and saw King David leaping and whirling before *Adonai*; and she despised him for it.

17] They brought in the Ark of *Adonai* and set it up in its place inside the tent which David had pitched for it, and David sacrificed burnt offerings and offerings of well-being before *Adonai.* **18]** When David finished sacrificing the burnt offerings and the offerings of well-being, he blessed the people in the name of *Adonai* of Hosts. **19]** And he distributed among all the people—the entire multitude of Israel, man and woman alike—to each a loaf of bread, a cake made in a pan, and a raisin cake. Then all the people left for their homes.

20] David went home to greet his household. And Michal daughter of Saul came out to meet David and said, "Didn't the king of Israel do himself honor today—exposing himself today in the sight of the slavegirls of his subjects, as one of the riffraff might expose himself!" **21]** David answered Michal, "It was before *Adonai* who chose me instead of your father and all his family and appointed me ruler over *Adonai*'s people Israel! I will dance before *Adonai* **22]** and dishonor myself even more and be low in my own esteem; but among the slavegirls that you speak of I will be honored."

(II Samuel 6:12-22)

By bringing the Ark of God into Jerusalem, David made Jerusalem the religious center of the Jewish people. How did he show his joy over this accomplishment? _____

_____

_____

_____

Michal, David's wife, despised David for leaping and whirling before *Adonai*. Assume the role of Michal and complete the following sentence.

"I was angry at my husband the king for acting so wildly in front of his subjects because _____

_____

_____

_____

Which of the following best expresses your opinion?

_____ 1. One should pray quietly and orderly.

_____ 2. When someone sings loudly and shows a lot of emotion during prayer, it is embarrassing to others.

_____ 3. Sometimes it feels good to pray enthusiastically and to sing loudly.

4. Other _____

_____

_____

After reading II Samuel 6:12-22, which of the leadership qualities you listed previously do you think apply to King David?

_____   _____   _____   _____   _____

The Prophet Nathan
Delivers a Message to David

As David becomes more settled in his role as king, he occasionally misuses his position of authority to get what he wants. An example of this is the case of Uriah and Bathsheba. David falls in love with Bathsheba, the wife of Uriah. In order to be able to marry Bathsheba, David sends Uriah off to battle, assigning him to a dangerous position in the front lines. Tragically, Uriah dies in a fierce battle, and Uriah's wife mourns for her husband. After the period of mourning is over, David sends for her and makes her his wife. God is not pleased with these actions of his anointed and sends the prophet Nathan to deliver the message. Nathan begins by telling a story.

Adonai was displeased with what David had done, **1]** and *Adonai* sent Nathan to David. He came to him and said, "There were two men in the same city, one rich and one poor. **2]** The rich man had very large flocks and herds, **3]** but the poor man had only one little ewe lamb that he had bought. He tended it and it grew up together with him and his children: it used to share his morsel of bread, drink from his cup, and nestle in his bosom; it was like a daughter to him. **4]** One day, a traveler came to the rich man, but he was loath to take anything from his own flocks or herds to prepare a meal for the guest who had come to him; so he took the poor man's lamb and prepared it for the man who had come to him."

5] David flew into a rage against the man, and said to Nathan, "As *Adonai* lives, the man who did this deserves to die! **6]** He shall pay for the lamb four times over, because he did such a thing and showed no pity." **7]** And Nathan said to David, "That man is you! Thus said *Adonai*, the God of Israel: `It was I who anointed you king over Israel and it was I who rescued you from the hand of Saul. **8]** I gave you your master's house and possession of your master's wives; and I gave you the House of Israel and Judah; and if that were not enough, I would give you twice as much more. **9]** Why then have you flouted the command of *Adonai* and done what displeases the Eternal? You have put Uriah the Hittite to the sword; you took his wife and made her your wife and had him killed by the sword of the Ammonites. **10]** Therefore the sword shall never depart from your House—because you spurned Me by taking the wife of Uriah the Hittite and making her your wife.' **11]** Thus said *Adonai*: 'I will make a calamity rise against you from within your own house; I will take your wives and give them to another man before your very eyes and he shall sleep with your wives under this very sun. **12]** You acted in secret, but I will make this happen in the sight of all Israel and in broad daylight.' "

13] David said to Nathan, "I stand guilty before *Adonai*!" And Nathan replied to David, "*Adonai* has remitted your sin; you shall not die. **14]** However, since you have spurned the enemies of *Adonai* by this deed, the child about to be born to you shall die."

(II Samuel 12:1-14)

II Samuel 12:1-14 teaches us a great deal. Which of these statements are facts found in the text, and which are lessons we can conclude from reading the text? After each statement, write either F (fact) or L (lesson).

God disapproves of David's behavior involving Bathsheba and Uriah. _____

Nathan's delivery of God's message is proof that prophets had the authority to admonish even a powerful king. _____

David is king because God appointed him. Therefore, David is still obligated to follow God's laws. _____

The sins of a human king are punished by God, the Supreme Ruler. _____

David's admission of wrongdoing leads to a lessening of his punishment. _____

CHAPTER

6 Summary

The texts you have studied in this chapter paint a portrait of one of the greatest figures of Jewish history, King David. The *Tanach* tells us more about David than about any other Jewish king. David grew from a simple shepherd to a powerful ruler who helped shape the future of the Jewish people by unifying them politically and spiritually. But David, like all human beings, had weaknesses and imperfections. And, when he placed his own selfish desires above the need to be fair and just, he had to answer to God for his actions.

The message of God's displeasure was delivered by Nathan. From the model of Nathan we learn about the role of the prophet as one who protests injustices and serves as a social conscience. In the next chapter we will explore two more dramatic examples of prophets and their roles in shaping the history of the Jewish people.

The Prophet Isaiah. *Michelangelo Buonarroti, fresco, 1512.*

NEVI'IM/PROPHETS:
The Prophet as Social Conscience

About This Chapter: In this chapter you will explore the role of the prophet. You will seek to understand the purpose of the prophets' words. Finally, you will search to find meaning for today in the messages delivered by the prophets over 2,500 years ago.

The Role of the Prophet

Today someone who feels the need to help society may decide to run for public office or join volunteer organizations. Others may choose such careers that center on helping society as the clergy, medicine, social work, science, education, or law. In biblical times, the people known for their roles in pointing out the community's problems and offering new courses of action were the prophets. Of course, there is an important difference between the prophets of the *Tanach* and the people who want to help society today. The *Tanach* tells us that God appointed each prophet to this role. The prophet's role was to deliver God's message and to serve as God's partner in the effort to help society improve. Therefore, the position required a sincere, moral, ethical person who was deeply devoted to God and the Children of Israel.

The Messages of the Prophets

The messages of the prophets cover a wide range of topics. Sometimes they focus on people's wrong doings in everyday activities, such as fairness in business. Other times they deal with the need for moral and ethical treatment of the poor. On some occasions the message concerns affairs of state, such as foreign policy suggestions. No matter what the topic, the prophets' messages always remind us that where right and wrong are concerned nothing is too small or unimportant in the eyes of God. The biblical prophets spoke about the times in which they lived. Their pleas for stopping corruption, for abolishing war, or for helping the needy addressed the very real concerns of their day. Nonetheless, much of what the prophets said continues to speak to the problems we face today.

* The triumph of King David in uniting all the tribes of Israel into one kingdom was short-lived. King Solomon, who followed David, could keep things together only as long as he was alive. By Isaiah's time the Jewish nation had long been divided between the kingdom of Judah, which included Jerusalem, and the larger but less stable kingdom of Israel. Isaiah lived in Jerusalem and addressed his words to the people of Judah.

Isaiah: Prophet of Righteousness

In 742 B.C.E., Isaiah received a call to prophecy. It was a time of growing prosperity and comfort for the kingdoms of Israel and Judah.* Yet, it was also a time when surrounding nations threatened to invade the kingdoms. Isaiah warns that wealth and prosperity for some people have led to a lack of concern for the less fortunate and to an increase in corruption. He presents God's protests against empty ritual acts and holiday celebrations that are not followed by righteous behavior.

11] "What need have I of all your sacrifices?"
Says *Adonai*.
"I am filled with burnt offerings of rams,
And fat of fed beasts,
And blood of bulls;
And I have no delight
In lambs and he-goats.
12] That you come to appear before Me—
Who asked that of you?
Trample My courts
13] no more;
Bringing offerings is futile,
Incense is offensive to Me.
New moon and sabbath,
Proclaiming of solemnities,
Assemblies of iniquity,
I cannot abide.
14] Your new moons and fixed seasons
Fill Me with loathing;
They are becoming a burden to Me,
I cannot endure them.
15] And when you lift up your hands,
I will turn My eyes away from you;
Though you pray at length,
I will not listen.
Your hands are stained with crime—
16] Wash yourselves clean;
Put your evil doings
Away from My sight.
Cease to do evil;
17] Learn to do good.
Devote yourselves to justice;
Aid the wronged.
Uphold the rights of the orphan;
Defend the cause of the widow. . . ."

(Isaiah 1:11-17)

In Chapter 3, *Vayikra*/Leviticus, we learned that, in ancient times, sacrifices were offered to God as a form of prayer. According to Isaiah 1:11-17, the sacrifices had become empty rituals, lacking in sincerity.

In what ways can prayer be insincere today?

Check the answer(s) with which you agree or, if you wish, add your own.

_____ 1. when people pray with their eyes on their watches to see when services will be over

_____ 2. when people rush through a Pesach seder as quickly as possible so they can get to the meal

_____ 3. when people read the words in the *siddur* ("prayer book") without thinking about what they really mean

_____ 4. when someone takes a napkin from the refreshments after Shabbat services and throws it on the ground

_____ 5. when someone sits and talks to a neighbor throughout services

6. other _____

_____

Listed below are the things that God told Isaiah to urge the people to do. All of these are still concerns today. Give examples of actions that you can take to fulfill these commands.

1. Learn to do good. _____

_____

_____

2. Devote yourself to justice. _____

_____

_____

3. Aid the wronged. _____

_____

_____

4. Uphold the rights of the orphan. _____

_____

_____

5. Defend the cause of the widow. _____

_____

_____

Jeremiah Lamenting the Fall of Jerusalem. *Rembrandt van Rijn, painting, 1630.*

Jeremiah: Prophet of Faith

Jeremiah, like Isaiah, lived in Judah. He took on the role of prophet around the year 626 B.C.E., more than one hundred years after Isaiah. Since Isaiah's time, much had changed and much had stayed the same. The period of prosperity had ended. Attacks from neighboring nations had become a reality. Still, the people lacked a complete commitment to the *berit* and to caring for one another. Oppression of the poor and helpless continued. And no one seemed to notice that the kingdom was on the verge of collapse. No one, that is, except for Jeremiah.

Jeremiah watches the progression of events with deep concern. He warns of the impending disaster, the fall of the kingdom of Judah, and the capture of its capital, Jerusalem, by the Babylonians. He pleads for the people to wake up to their fate. He cries out, ". . .My heart moans within me,/I cannot be silent;/For I hear the blare of horns,/Alarms of war./Disaster overtakes disaster. . . ." (Jeremiah 4:19-20) But no one listens to Jeremiah's warnings. The people disappoint him because they "are stupid,/They give Me no heed;/They are foolish children,/They are not intelligent./They are clever at doing wrong,/But unable to do right." (Jeremiah 4:22) Jeremiah's frustration grows when he looks around and sees not only a society of foolish people but also a ruler, Shallum, son of Josiah of Judah, also known as Jehoahaz, who emphasizes material riches over caring for the needy.

13] Ha! he who builds his house with unfairness
And his upper chambers with injustice,
Who makes his fellowman work without pay
And does not give him his wages,
14] Who thinks: I will build me a vast palace
With spacious upper chambers,
Provided with windows,
Paneled in cedar,
Painted in vermilion!
15] Do you think you are more a king
Because you compete in cedar?
Your father ate and drank
And dispensed justice and equity—
Then all went well with him.
16] He upheld the rights of the poor and needy—
Then all was well.
That is truly heeding Me
                                            — declares *Adonai*.
17] But your eyes and your mind are only
On ill-gotten gains,
On shedding the blood of the innocent,
On committing fraud and violence.

(*Jeremiah* 22:13-17)

Match the ills of society listed by Jeremiah with similar ills in the world today.

A. who makes his fellowman work without pay

____ 1. people who are concerned with "keeping up" with the neighbors—building bigger and bigger houses

B. who thinks: I will build me a vast palace with spacious upper chambers

____ 2. deaths of innocent bystanders who get caught in the violence of the streets

C. your eyes and your mind are only on ill-gotten gains

____ 3. employers who pay low wages and take advantage of people who cannot find other jobs

D. shedding the blood of the innocent, on committing fraud and violence

____ 4. people who get rich by cheating others

The prophets place special importance on the need for sharing with those who are in need. One way you can share with others less fortunate than you is to give to *tzedakah* a portion of the money you may receive for your birthday or bar/bat mitzvah. (*Tzedakah* means "righteousness." When we give money to others or to causes that can use our help, we are doing acts of righteousness.) What are the cause(s) to which you would like to donate some money. Write your choice and explain it.

_____

_____

_____

_____

_____

_____

_____

_____

_____

_____

Jeremiah witnesses the collapse of the kingdom of Judah and the destruction of Solomon's Temple in Jerusalem. He laments the people's exile from their homeland to Babylon. Yet, in the midst of disaster, he still manages to deliver God's message of hope.

31] See, a time is coming—declares *Adonai*—when I will make a new covenant with the House of Israel and the House of Judah. 32] It will not be like the covenant I made with their fathers, when I took them by the hand to lead them out of the land of Egypt, a covenant which they broke, so that I rejected them—declares *Adonai*. 33] But such is the covenant I will make with the House of Israel after these days—declares *Adonai*: I will put My Teaching into their inmost being and inscribe it upon their hearts. Then I will be their God, and they shall be My people. 34] No longer will they need to teach one another and say to one another, "Heed *Adonai*"; for all of them, from the least of them to the greatest, shall heed Me—declares *Adonai*.

> For I will forgive their iniquities,
> And remember their sins no more.

(Jeremiah 31:31-34)

ACTIVITIES

Which of the following adjectives would you use to describe the words of God in Jeremiah 31:31-34? Circle as many as you like.

hopeful	threatening	angry	forgiving
sincere	trusting	reassuring	

In Jeremiah we read the words of God: "... I will make a new covenant with the House of Israel and the House of Judah." How can the covenant be renewed?

_____

_____

In what ways do you think this new covenant will be different from the covenant made with Abraham, Isaac, and Jacob? (Review Chapter 1, *Bereshit*/Genesis, in this book for ideas.)

_____

_____

73

Read the two verses below. Then check the statement you think best expresses the main idea of the verses.

> I will put My Teaching into their inmost being and inscribe it upon their hearts. (Jeremiah 31:33)
>
> You shall love *Adonai* your God with all your heart. (Deuteronomy 6:5)

_____ Love of God is very important.

_____ The commandments of God should be with us at all times.

_____ True devotion to God comes from the heart.

_____ We should remember that we are Jews at all times.

The Messianic Era

The writings of the prophets often talk about a time when there will be no pain, war, disease, or other types of suffering. This period of harmony is called the Messianic Era. Messianic comes from the word "messiah." The Hebrew word for Messiah is *Mashiach*, which means a person chosen by God to help bring about this new world order. Every year at the Pesach seder we open the door for Elijah as a symbol of our hope that the Messianic Era will come soon, bringing a time of harmony for all.

The Peaceable Kingdom. *Edward Hicks, painting, 1830-1840, based on the prophetic vision of a Messianic Era.*

Worcester Art Museum, Massachusetts

In the verses below, Isaiah offers one description of the Messianic Era.

6] The wolf shall dwell with the lamb,
The leopard lie down with the kid;
The calf, the beast of prey, and the fatling together,
With a little boy to herd them.
7] The cow and the bear shall graze,
Their young shall lie down together;
And the lion, like the ox, shall eat straw.
8] A babe shall play
Over a viper's hole,
And an infant pass his hand
Over an adder's den.
9] In all of My sacred mount
Nothing evil or vile shall be done;
For the land shall be filled with devotion to *Adonai*
As water covers the sea.   (Isaiah 11:6-9)

ACTIVITIES

In this vision does it say who will bring about this state of peace and harmony? Explain, with your own ideas, how you think the Messianic Era will come about. _____

_____

_____

The wolf shall dwell with the lamb,
The leopard lie down with the kid;...   Isaiah 11:6

And they shall beat their swords into plowshares
And their spears into pruning hooks:
Nation shall not take up
Sword against nation;
They shall never again know war.   Isaiah 2:4

. . .They shall follow My rules and faithfully obey My laws. Thus
they shall remain in the land which I gave to My servant Jacob and
in which your father dwelt; they and their children and their
children's children shall dwell there forever. . . .   Ezekiel 37:24, 25

These are three different visions of the Messianic Era. Tell which vision you like the most and why. Or describe your own vision of the peace that will be brought about by the coming of the Messiah._____

_____

_____

In the *Tanach* God communicated directly with the prophets. While God may no longer communicate in the same way today, there are people who have "prophetic vision." In other words, there are people who feel a need to speak out against the ills of society and work to improve the lives of all. Can you think of an example of such a person, living or dead? Explain what this person does or did for others. _____

_____

_____

_____

_____

CHAPTER

7 Summary

The task of the prophet was a difficult one. Being a person who reminded society of its wrongs was not a very popular position. It is no wonder that not every prophet readily agreed to take on the responsibility without first needing a little encouragement from God. But, ultimately, all the prophets spoke up honestly and emphatically about the ills of society and the need for change. The prophets complimented the people when it was appropriate, but more often they criticized them for their selfish behavior, for ignoring the needs of the poor, and for failing to uphold the *berit* between the Jewish people and God.

The prophets were the conscience of society. They reminded the people that, even if wrongs were not committed by everyone, it was still everyone's responsibility to work toward building and maintaining a just and righteous community. And it is the voice of the prophets that continues to speak to us today, urging us to live upright, caring lives.

8 KETUVIM/WRITINGS:
Psalms and Proverbs

About This Chapter: This chapter focuses on two books from the third and final section of the *Tanach, Ketuvim.* Both the Book of Psalms and the Book of Proverbs offer us beautifully worded expressions on how to live and how to treat our fellow human beings.

King David Plays the Harp as the Ark Is Brought into Jerusalem.

M.638, f.39v. Courtesy of the Pierpont Morgan Library, New York

The Poetry of the Psalms

The *Tanach* is filled with poetry. You looked at poetry from the Torah, the Five Books of Moses, when you studied the Song at the Sea (*Shemot*/Exodus 15); and you examined examples of the poetic words of *Nevi'im*/Prophets in the excerpts from Isaiah and Jeremiah. Now you will look at excerpts from an entire book of poetry, the first of the thirteen books of *Ketuvim*/Writings, Psalms, known in Hebrew as *Tehilim.*

Psalms is a collection of beautiful poems that are over 2,000 years old. It includes a total of one hundred and fifty psalms. Some of them celebrate God's greatness. Others focus on God's role as the Sovereign of the universe. Another group of psalms lament the misfortune of the Jews or the personal suffering of individuals. A special feature of many of the laments is an expression of certainty that God will hear prayers and answer them. There are also psalms of thanksgiving and psalms that emphasize types of behavior that please God. As you read and explore the following selections from the Book of Psalms, see if you can identify which of these descriptions fits each of these psalms.

* While the exact authorship of all the psalms is not known, tradition states that King David is the author of the Book of Psalms. For this reason many of the psalms begin with "A psalm of David."

23 A psalm of David.*

1] *Adonai* is my shepherd;
     I shall not want.
2] *Adonai* makes me lie down in green pastures;
     God leads me beside the still waters.
3] God renews my life;
     God guides me in straight paths
     as befits the name of God.
4] Though I walk through a valley of deepest darkness,
     I fear no harm, for You are with me;
     Your rod and Your staff—they comfort me.
5] You prepare a table for me in full view of my enemies;
     You anoint my head with oil;
     my drink overflows.
6] Surely goodness and steadfast love shall follow me
     all the days of my life,
     and I shall dwell in the house of *Adonai*
     forever.

ACTIVITIES

Which of the different themes below do you think is expressed in Psalm 23? Check as many as you want.

____ the greatness of God   ____ God as Sovereign

____ lament of national suffering   ____ thanksgiving

____ lament of personal suffering   ____ confidence that prayers will be heard

____ behavior pleasing to God

Psalm 23 is often recited along with other prayers as a request for God to bring a speedy recovery to someone who is ill. Also it is frequently read during funerals. Which do you think is a more appropriate use of this psalm, as a prayer for health or a prayer for a person who has died? _____

_____

ACTIVITIES (CONTINUED)

Explain your answer. _____

_____

_____

150 Hallelujah.

1] Praise God in God's sanctuary;
   praise God in the sky, God's stronghold.
2] Praise God for God's mighty acts;
   praise God for God's exceeding greatness.
3] Praise God with blasts of the horn;
   praise God with harp and lyre.
4] Praise God with timbrel and dance;
   praise God with lute and pipe.
5] Praise God with resounding cymbals;
   praise God with loud-clashing cymbals.
6] Let all that breathes praise *Adonai*.
   Hallelujah.

ACTIVITY

Rewrite Psalm 150, using your own words and ideas about how to praise God.

1] Praise God in (*name a place*) _____
   praise God in (*name a place*) _____
2] Praise God for (*name an action*) _____
   praise God for (*name an action*) _____
3] Praise God with (*name an instrument*) _____
   praise God with (*name an instrument*) _____
4] Praise God with (*name another instrument*) _____
   praise God with (*name another instrument*) _____
5] Praise God with (*name another instrument*) _____
   praise God with (*repeat the name of the instrument*) _____
6] Let all that breathes praise *Adonai*.
   Hallelujah.

15 A psalm of David.

1] *Adonai*, who may visit in Your tent,
who may dwell on Your holy mountain?

2] The person who lives without blame,
who does what is right,
whose heart acknowledges the truth;

3] whose tongue is not given to evil;
who has never done harm to others,
or borne reproach for [acts toward] neighbors;

4] for whom a contemptible person is abhorrent,
but who honors those who fear *Adonai*;
who stands by oaths even to one's own hurt;

5] who has never lent money at interest,
or accepted a bribe against the innocent.

The person who acts thus shall never be shaken.

ACTIVITIES

Psalm 15 puts forth quite a number of ways a person should behave to be close to God. Rank these, according to your opinion, in the order of their importance.

_____ 1. not to harm others

_____ 2. to act honestly and fairly towards others

_____ 3. to be honest to yourself

_____ 4. not to tell lies or gossip

_____ 5. not to associate with mean, nasty people

_____ 6. to give honor to people who deserve it

_____ 7. to keep a promise

_____ 8. not to take financial advantage of others

_____ 9. to refuse to accept bribes

Which of the above do you think is the most difficult to perform? Why?

_____

_____

_____

The Wisdom of the Proverbs

The aim of the second book of *Ketuvim*/Writings, Proverbs, is to help guide us toward moral and ethical behavior. While it is true that this is the aim of much of the *Tanach*, Proverbs can be viewed as a special handbook for living a moral and religious life. The word "proverb" usually refers to a short statement of folk wisdom. However, the Hebrew name for the Book of Proverbs, *Mishle*, goes beyond this simple definition. In the Book of Proverbs we encounter sayings of truth, sayings with hidden meanings, parables, and even riddles.

Like the Book of Psalms, the Book of Proverbs dates back over 2,000 years. Also, like Psalms, the author of Proverbs is unknown although tradition claims that King Solomon, son of King David, wrote this book.

According to tradition, King Solomon wrote the Book of Proverbs.

Gustave Doré, France, 1865

Solomon.

Another similarity between the two books is the richness of ideas and thoughts found in them. You can open up a *Tanach* to any of the thirty-one chapters of Proverbs and find verses of great wisdom as well as common sense.

Let's look at just a few.

False scales are an abomination to *Adonai*;/An honest weight pleases God.   (Proverbs 11:1)

A base person gives away secrets, /But a trustworthy soul keeps a confidence.   (11:13)

A person who has regard for life pays regard to commandments....   (19:16)

Do not love sleep lest you be impoverished....   (20:13)

The plans of the diligent make only for gain;/All rash haste makes only for loss.   (21:5)

Let the mouth of another praise you, not yours,/The lips of a stranger, not your own.   (27:2)

Better is a poor person who lives blamelessly
Than a rich person whose ways are crooked.   (28:6)

An intelligent child heeds instruction,
But a child who keeps company with gluttons disgraces a parent.   (28:7)

ACTIVITY

Write the chapter and verse from the Book of Proverbs of the thought that is also expressed in the statements below.

1. Early to bed and early to rise make a person healthy, wealthy, and wise.   _____

2. A person of poor character cannot keep secrets.   _____

3. Compliments should come from someone else.   _____

4. A parent is honored by a child who studies hard and avoids contact with kids who could be a bad influence.   _____

5. God is concerned with our actions in every aspect of our lives—prayer, work, business.   _____

6. Careful planning leads to success while
   haste makes waste.   _____

7. It does not matter if you are rich or poor.
   What matters is that you live a good, honest life.   _____

8. Living life with respect means giving honor
   to the *mitzvot*.   _____

CHAPTER

8 Summary

This chapter concludes our study of the *Tanach*. In this chapter, you have learned about the poetry in the Book of Psalms and the wisdom in the Book of Proverbs. You discovered the messages of a selection of psalms, and you interpreted the meaning of a variety of proverbs. But, like the chapters on the Five Books of Moses, you must remember that there is much more to *Nevi'im* and *Ketuvim* than you have covered here. Hopefully this beginning exploration will encourage you to delve into the books of the *Tanach* in further depth in the future.

Our sacred texts go beyond the *Tanach*. There are fascinating books of Jewish law that expand and comment on the content of the *Tanach*. There are wonderful books of legends that attempt to unlock the messages behind the written words of the *Tanach*. In the coming chapters you will be introduced to these texts and given the opportunity to sample excerpts from these books that form the foundation of Judaism as we know it today.

Moses Coming Down from Mount Sinai.

84

Rabbinic Literature

About This Unit: The Judaism we practice today is not exactly the same as the religion described in the Torah, the Five Books of Moses. How, when, and why did it change? What are the differences? What is the Oral Law, and what influences does it have on the Jewish religion today? In this unit you will explore these questions.

Written Law and Oral Law: Our Two Traditions

In Chapter 2, *Shemot*/Exodus, you read about the Jewish people's dramatic experience at Mount Sinai. According to Jewish teaching, as recorded in the Bible, God gave the Torah to Moses, and Moses transmitted it to the Children of Israel. When we look at the *mitzvot* of the Torah, we see that many center on the life of the Israelites as a nomadic community living in the desert.

Yet, as the Children of Israel became a more settled people living in agricultural communities or in cities, the laws of the Torah did not as clearly address their everyday lives. Slowly, over time, a need grew for the laws to be expanded upon and interpreted in ways that fit the changing living situations of the Jewish people. The job of keeping Judaism alive and flexible enough to address these new types of communities fell upon wise and scholarly people called rabbis.

The rabbis carefully studied the Torah in light of the changing circumstances of the people's lives. They began to develop an Oral Law. The aim of the Oral Law was to expand on, interpret, and seek new meaning in the *mitzvot* of the Written Law, the Torah. The Oral Law gets its name from the fact that, for a very long time, it was transmitted orally. Why and when it came to be written down will be discussed later.

According to the rabbis, they were not creating anything new by developing the Oral Law. The rabbis felt that their skill rested in their ability to uncover meanings and interpretations already in the Torah.

The rabbis explained the unfolding of the Oral Law in this way: Moses received Torah from God in two parts. One part was in writing and the other, which was not written down, was given orally for Moses to memorize. Both the Written Law and the Oral Law were handed down from Moses to the next generation and on to the next generation and so on.

It is not hard to imagine how something written could be passed down. But what about the Oral Law? How was it transmitted from one age to the next? A story from the rabbis describes the importance of the oral teachings. It also presents their view of how oral teachings are passed from generation to generation.

A non-Jew came to the famous and respected Rabbi Hillel and said, "I will become a Jew on the basis of the Written Law. I believe that. But I will not accept the Oral Law. I cannot trust it. It seems like a mere invention to me."

Hillel said, "OK. I will give you lessons so that you may become a Jew. I will begin with the Written Law. This is your first lesson. Here are the first letters of the Hebrew alphabet: *alef, bet, gimel, dalet.* Study these letters and then come back tomorrow and repeat this lesson for me."

The next day the student came back, and Hillel said to him, "Recite yesterday's lesson."

The student said, "*Alef, bet, gimel, dalet.*"

Hillel said, "No, it should be *dalet, gimel, bet, alef.*"

The astonished student said, "But yesterday you taught me *alef, bet, gimel, dalet.*"

And Hillel said, "You are recalling my oral teaching of yesterday. You believed me when I taught you, just as I believed my own teacher, and he believed his."

We get two important messages from this story. The first message is a reminder that we learn a great deal in life by listening to others. Listening to the oral teachings of others is how we learn before we even know how to read. We continue to learn orally throughout our lives.

The second message of the story is that Jewish teaching is based on the very special relationship that exists between a teacher and a student. The rabbis taught that one respected and wise teacher taught all he knew to one pupil and that pupil became a teacher and taught it to his pupil and so on. This process of teaching began with Moses, who passed the teachings on in an unbroken chain from one generation to the next on to our day.

The Mishnah

The first point about the Oral Law is that after hundreds of years of being transmitted orally it was written down in book form. Around 200 C.E., a very well-known and highly respected leader, Rabbi Judah Ha-Nasi, organized into written form a large collection of the oral teachings. These oral teachings were developed by rabbis called *tannaim.* The book compiled by Rabbi Judah Ha-Nasi is called the *Mishnah.* We do not know the exact reasons for his undertaking this task, but, by studying the dramatic historical times in which he lived, we can come up with some very likely answers.

One hundred and thirty years before, in 70 C.E., the holy Temple in Jerusalem had been destroyed. This meant that the center of Jewish religion no longer existed. How was Judaism to go on? How could the holidays be celebrated without a place to bring sacrifices to God? Where and how were Jews supposed to worship?

One very wise and forward-thinking man, Rabbi Yochanan ben Zakkai, led the way to answering these and many other questions. He saw the Temple in ruins and knew that, for Judaism to survive, something had to be done. So he established the first formal center of Jewish study. Yochanan ben Zakkai was committed to developing the Oral Law. Over the next century others followed his example of reshaping Judaism to fit the tremendous changes of the times.

Judah Ha-Nasi came along and undertook the task of collecting the *tannaim's* teachings into the *Mishnah.* Through his work, Judah Ha-Nasi expanded the guidelines for living as a Jew and contributed to the continuing survival of Judaism and the Jewish people. By compiling the various versions of the Oral Law that existed during his lifetime, Judah Ha-Nasi not only gave the Oral Law a uniform structure and organization but also provided a uniform structure and organization for the Jewish community. Also, by providing a written version of the Oral Law, Judah Ha-Nasi helped reduce internal disagreements within the Jewish community. Finally, Judah Ha-Nasi's efforts made the Jewish community stronger and more unified. This in turn lessened the threats from the ruling Roman government, which sought to weaken the Jewish community and Judaism.

The Talmud and the Gemara

Once Rabbi Judah Ha-Nasi had organized the Oral Law in a systematic manner, it became much easier to study and follow. The sages, known as *amoraim*, devoted themselves to the study of the *Mishnah*. All their studying and interpreting of the *Mishnah* resulted in the creation of another much larger collection of rabbinic teachings called the *Gemara*. The combination of the *Mishnah* and the *Gemara* make up the two main parts of the Talmud. In the Talmud, first a paragraph from the *Mishnah* is presented. It is followed by further interpretations and discussions in the *Gemara*.

The study of the *Mishnah* took place in two different locations: the Land of Israel and Babylonia (which corresponds to a part of modern Iraq). Therefore, there are two different collections called Talmud. At the time of the appearance of the *Mishnah* (about 200 C.E.), there were two main centers of Jewish learning. The smaller center was in the Land of Israel because the Jewish population of the Land of Israel had shrunk after the destruction of the Second Temple in 70 C.E. and the unsuccessful Jewish revolt of 135 C.E. In order to escape the oppression of the rulers in Israel, a great number of the Jews left to live in Babylonia. The Talmud produced by the *amoraim* of the Land of Israel is called the Palestinian Talmud or the *Talmud Yerushalmi*. It was completed around 400 C.E.

The Jews who moved to Babylonia established many academies of Jewish learning. And the Talmud produced by the growing Jewish community of Babylonia is known as the Babylonian Talmud or the *Talmud Bavli*. It was completed around 500 C.E. As the Jewish population of Babylonia grew, so did the importance of its academies of Jewish learning. And eventually the *Talmud Bavli* came to have greater authority than the *Talmud Yerushalmi*.

The Midrash

There is one more very important component to rabbinic literature: the Midrash. The Midrash, like the

Mishnah, responded to changing circumstances and made the Torah come alive in new ways. There are two main types of *midrash*: *midrash halachah*, which focuses on matters of Jewish law, and *midrash aggadah*, which is primarily concerned with nonlegal matters. The uniqueness of the *midrash aggadah* is that its primary format for searching, examining, and investigating the meaning of the *Tanach* is through telling wonderfully imaginative and interesting stories. The *midrashim* (plural for *midrash*) you will study in this book will all be *midrash aggadah*. Sometimes a *midrash* tries to fill in the gaps that seem to exist in the text of the *Tanach*. *For example*: The Torah does not tell us about Isaac's feelings after he was almost sacrificed by his father, Abraham. But many *midrashim* do. Or what did Cain and Abel say to each other before Cain killed Abel? The Torah does not give us their conversation, but several *midrashim* offer a rich array of answers.

There are many different collections of *midrashim* that were gathered and organized into written form. However, unlike the *Mishnah* and the Talmud, there is no one single book or set of books called the Midrash. One similarity between the Midrash and the *Mishnah* is that, long before they were written down, they were both part of a rich tradition of oral teachings shared from generation to generation. The collections of *midrashim* that do exist include many of the those created between 100-1200 C.E. This period is considered to be the height of the development of *midrashim*, but the tradition of creating *midrashim* continues to this day.

Unit Three: Summary

Most of the earlier chapters of this book have covered parts of the Written Law or the Torah. In this unit you have been introduced to some of the details of the Oral Law of Judaism. The three types of oral teachings briefly described here—*Mishnah, Gemara*, and Midrash—are referred to as rabbinic literature. These oral teachings represent the wisdom of many rabbis, who devoted their lives to Jewish learning and teaching. These rabbis were dedicated to the idea that, for Judaism to live, it must adjust to the changing circumstances in the lives of the Jewish people. Their development of new understandings of how to live as Jews emphasizes the richness of Judaism and its ability to grow and evolve with the times. The efforts of the rabbis enhanced and enriched the Judaism of the Torah and laid the foundation for Judaism as we know and live it today.

Rabbi Judah Ha-Nasi, *the editor of the* Mishnah.

CHAPTER 9

THE MISHNAH

About This Chapter: You have now learned some of the background behind the development of the rabbinic literature. Now you will have the opportunity to examine some selections from the *Mishnah*. As you read, pay attention to the types of issues the *Mishnah* addresses and how the *Mishnah* helps clarify the *mitzvot* of the Torah.

The Making of the Mishnah

Mishnah means "to teach" or "to learn." The *Mishnah*, as you read previously, is a fascinating collection of the oral teachings of rabbis known as the *tannaim*. The teachings of the *Mishnah* focus on matters of *halachah* ("system of Jewish law"). The *Mishnah* works by taking the *mitzvot* of the *Tanach* and interpreting them. The *Mishnah* offers guidelines for following the *mitzvot*. *For example:* You know that in Exodus we find the *mitzvah* "*Remember* the sabbath day and keep it holy. Six days you shall labor and do all your work, but the seventh day is a sabbath of *Adonai* your God: you shall not do any work. . . . " (*Shemot*/Exodus 20:8-10) Just exactly what are we to do to *remember* the Sabbath day? What are we permitted to do on the Sabbath day? What are we not permitted to do? These are the types of concrete practices that the rabbis of the *Mishnah* address. In other words, the goal of the *Mishnah* is to teach us how to live according to Jewish law.*

Rabbi Judah Ha-Nasi (late 2nd-early 3rd centuries C.E.) undertook an awesome task when he compiled the *Mishnah*. He took the expansions, explanations, and clarifications of Jewish law that for generations had been orally transmitted and categorized them into six divisions or orders (*sedarim* סְדָרִים). Each order is subdivided into sections called tractates (*massechtot* מַסֶּכְתּוֹת). The tractates are divided into chapters (*perakim* פְּרָקִים), and the chapters are divided into paragraphs (*mishnayot* מִשְׁנָיוֹת). The Hebrew word for one paragraph is *mishnah* מִשְׁנָה . So both the whole collection and the individual paragraphs have the same name, *Mishnah*.

* Halachah *is the Hebrew word for "Jewish law." It comes from the word "to walk" or the "way in which one should walk." Thus by following* halachah *one will walk in the right way or live a life according to Jewish law.*

Contents of the Mishnah

Each of the six orders of the *Mishnah* has a title. The titles tell about the general contents of the orders. The titles of the orders are:

1. *Zeraim* — Seeds
2. *Moed* — Festivals
3. *Nashim* — Women
4. *Nezikin* — Damages
5. *Kodashim* — Sacred Things
6. *Toharot* — Ritual Cleanness

These six orders of the *Mishnah* cover all aspects of life. Both Jewish Written Law and Oral Law, do not categorize life according to religious and nonreligious actions. All life is thought to be religious because all our actions have the potential to move us closer to God.

The *Mishnah*, which is a code for living a religious life, includes topics ranging from everyday activities (*example*: what to do when you find an unclaimed object) to special ritual activities (*example*: the proper way to celebrate a holiday). Furthermore, because Judah Ha-Nasi wanted to make sure that every part of Jewish law was included in the *Mishnah*, laws dealing even with Temple sacrifices are included. These were included despite the fact that sacrifices were no longer in practice by the time the *Mishnah* was compiled.

The *Mishnah* is written in a compact style without a lot of extra detail. Sometimes when you read the *Mishnah*, you get the impression that people who lived at the time it was written must have had a clearer understanding of what was going on than we do today. Yet, with a little practice, the text of the *mishnayot* slowly begins to unfold and make sense. We are going to turn now to a few *Mishnah* sample selections. Some include the rabbis' discussions on a particular legal point. Others offer interpretations of specific Torah verses. We will begin with some familiar lines from *Shemot*/Exodus and then see how the *Mishnah* works to interpret and expand on them.

How Should We Observe Shabbat?

Our earliest lessons about Shabbat come from the Torah. In *Bereshit*/Genesis 2:3, we read that ". . . God blessed the seventh day and declared it holy, because on it God ceased from all the work of creation . . . ." Later we read the following in *Shemot*/Exodus 20:8-10:

8] Remember the sabbath day and keep it holy. **9]** Six days you shall labor and do all your work, **10]** but the seventh day is a sabbath of *Adonai* your God: you shall not do any work—you, your son or daughter, your male or female slave, or your cattle, or the stranger who is within your settlements.

While the *Shemot* passage offers more details than *Bereshit* 2:3, it also raises quite a number of questions: What kind of activities qualify as "work"? Are parents responsible for making sure that their children do not work on the Sabbath for the entire lifetime of their sons and daughters? To what degree do the rules of keeping the Sabbath apply to non-Jews? Are there times when the rules for keeping the Sabbath can be broken?

The second order of the *Mishnah, Moed*—Festivals, begins with Tractate *Shabbat*. The twenty-four chapters of Tractate *Shabbat* address the many questions and interpretations that grow out of studying these verses from Exodus. Below are a few examples of *mishnayot* from Tractate *Shabbat*. As you read them, try to figure out the questions they are concerned with answering.

7.2 The main classes of work are forty save one: sowing, plowing, reaping, binding sheaves, threshing, winnowing, cleansing crops, grinding, sifting, kneading, baking, shearing wool, washing or beating or dyeing it [wool], spinning, weaving, making two loops, weaving two threads, separating two threads, tying a [knot], loosening a [knot], sewing two stitches, tearing in order to sew two stitches, hunting a gazelle, slaughtering or flaying or salting it [a gazelle] or curing its skin, scraping it or cutting it up, writing two letters, erasing in order to write two letters, building, pulling down, putting out a fire, lighting a fire, striking with a hammer, and taking out anything from one domain into another [carrying objects from the private space of your home to a public area].

16.1 Any of the scrolls of the *Tanach* may be saved from burning [even if it is necessary to break the rules against carrying on Shabbat] . . . .

16.6 If a gentile came to put out the fire [on Shabbat], the Jews may not say to him, "Put it out" or "Do not put it out," since Jews are not responsible for making sure that a non-Jew keeps Shabbat. But, if a minor [Jewish child under thirteen] comes to put out the fire, the Jewish adults may not permit him to do so since the adults are responsible for making sure that Jewish children keep Shabbat.

ACTIVITY

Each of these three examples of *mishnayot* deals with aspects of the *mitzvah* to "remember the sabbath day and make it holy."

Next to the ideas listed below, write the number of the *mishnah* (7.2, 16.1, or 16.6) from which it comes.

1. The scrolls of the Torah are so precious to us that we may break the rules of Shabbat to save them from a fire. _____

2. Building is one of the types of work prohibited on Shabbat. _____

3. Parents are responsible for guiding their children in the ways of following the *mitzvot* until the children turn thirteen. After reaching thirteen, the age of bar/bat mitzvah, children are responsible for their own actions. _____

4. The *mishnah* includes among its thirty-nine types of work prohibited on Shabbat many activities connected to agriculture. _____

The Study of Torah

By now you know that our sacred texts are full of *mitzvot* for us to follow. By working to fulfill the *mitzvot*, we hope to lead better, enriched lives. But what exactly are the rewards of performing *mitzvot*? (*For example*: If you do something nice for a friend, do you get anything out of it?) What about times when it is hard to perform a *mitzvah*? What makes you go ahead and do it? In the first order of the *Mishnah*, *Zeraim* — Seeds, Tractate *Peah*, the rabbis offer us some guidance on these questions.

> 1.1 These are the deeds [*mitzvot*] for which there is no prescribed measure: leaving crops at the corner of a field for the poor; offering first fruits as a gift to the Temple; bringing special offerings to the Temple on the Three Festivals [Sukot, Pesach, Shavuot]; doing deeds of loving-kindness; and the study of the Torah. These are the deeds which yield immediate fruit [reward] and continue to yield fruit in time to come: honoring father and mother, deeds of loving-kindness, making peace between one person and another. And the study of Torah is equal to all of them.

ACTIVITIES

The first part of this *mishnah* states that there is "no prescribed measure" for these *mitzvot*, and then it lists the *mitzvot*. What exactly do you think "no prescribed measure" means? Complete *one* of the two sentences below.

1. "No prescribed measure" means that you get credit for following these *mitzvot* even if you make just a little effort. I agree with this interpretation because _____

   _____

2. "No prescribed measure" means that you can always make more effort towards fulfilling any of these *mitzvot*. I agree with this interpretation because _____

   _____

Below is a list of the *mitzvot* that have no prescribed measure.
Choose the one that is most important to *you* and explain why.

1. helping the poor (leaving crops at the corner of the field)
2. giving thanks to God (offering first fruits)
3. participating in community worship (gathering at the Temple for the Three Festivals)
4. doing deeds of loving-kindness
5. study of Torah

_____

_____

The second part of this *mishnah* from *Peah* 1.1 discusses *mitzvot* that will reward us in this life and in time to come. What is the answer this *mishnah* gives to the question "Do some commandments hold greater weight than others?" _____

_____

What do the closing words from *Peah* 1.1 mean to you? "And the study of Torah is equal to all of them." Check the interpretation you think makes the most sense. Be prepared to explain your choice.

_____ 1. The only *mitzvah* we really have to do is to study Torah
_____ 2. Honoring father and mother is as important as the study of Torah
_____ 3. Deeds of loving-kindness can take the place of studying Torah
_____ 4. The study of Torah will lead us to performing all the other *mitzvot*

Fairness in Business and More

The *Mishnah* is concerned with all aspects of life. The following selection is an example. You will see how a *mishnah* can use one point as a jumping-off place for teaching another important lesson. This *mishnah* comes from *Nezikin* — Damages, Tractate *Baba Metzia* ("Middle Gate"). It begins as a discussion of business dealings in which one person may claim that the other cheated him but ends up at a quite different place.

4.10 As one may be guilty of wrongdoing in buying and selling, so may one be guilty of wrongdoing in words. One should not ask [a storekeeper]: "How much is this object?" knowing that he does not want to buy it. If there is a person who has repented from former wrongdoing, one must not say to him: "Remember what you did before!" If someone is descended from converts to Judaism, one must not say to him: "Remember the actions of your ancestors," for it is written: "You shall not wrong a stranger or oppress him, [for you were strangers in the land of Egypt]." (Exodus 22:20)

ACTIVITY

Let's try to sort out the various teachings of this *mishnah*. Put in order the sentences below so that they match up with the flow of the ideas in the *mishnah Baba Metzia* 4:10. Write a 1 next to the sentence that you think should go first and so on. (*Hint*: There are a few additional sentences offered here to link the ideas in the *mishnah*.)

_____ Asking a merchant how much something costs when you have no intention of buying it cheats him out of time that he could be spending with another customer and cheats him into thinking that you are a serious customer.

_____ It is not right to say to someone who has done *teshuvah* (asked for forgiveness for wrongdoings and promised not to do them again), "Don't forget all the bad things you did in the past."

_____ Cheating in business can be done through words as much as through actions.

_____ Another example of inappropriate things to say is to remind someone whose ancestors converted to Judaism, "Remember your ancestors did not always follow the ways of Judaism."

_____ Just as we should be careful of how we speak in business transactions, we should be careful when we speak to others in nonbusiness matters.

_____ We know that it is wrong to be rude and mean to people whose ancestors converted to Judaism because the Torah tells us that we know what it is like to be outsiders and to be oppressed, from our experiences of being strangers or foreigners who were oppressed in Egypt. For this reason we should make sure we do not treat others the way we were treated in Egypt.

9 Summary

In this chapter you have been introduced to the structure and content of the *Mishnah*. You looked at several different *Mishnah* selections, reflecting the wide range of topics it covers. You examined *mishnayot* that directly refer to Torah verses and others that state the law without mentioning Torah passages. From these examples you began to see how the *Mishnah* operates as a guide for Jewish living. You also saw from these selections that, while the language of the *Mishnah* may be short and simple, it is not always easy to understand.

After the *Mishnah* was compiled, those who studied it rapidly began to expand on and further interpret it. The result of this was the creation of yet another much larger collection of Jewish law known as the Talmud. In the next chapter you will explore the world of the *Gemara*, the part of the Talmud that comments on and interprets the *Mishnah*.

10 THE TALMUD

About This Chapter: Even though the writing down of the *Mishnah* was a tremendous feat it was really only a beginning. The *Mishnah* soon became the focus of study for rabbis and scholars. Their discussions, interpretations, and expansions were eventually organized into the *Gemara*. In this chapter you will look at some *Gemara* selections, all from the Babylonian Talmud. During your examination you will try to figure out the goal of the rabbis' efforts.

From Mishnah to Gemara

In many ways the *Mishnah* was quite difficult to follow. Because the *Mishnah* was originally oral, it was intentionally short on details and explanations. This made it easier to learn and to transmit to others. But, once it was written down, the style of the *Mishnah* presented many problems. So the rabbis carefully studied the *Mishnah* and came up with commentaries and interpretations of the *Mishnah*.

First, the rabbis clarified confusing passages. Once this was accomplished, they tried to figure out how the laws of the *Mishnah* were developed by looking for underlying rules that connected the laws. The rabbis also expanded the Mishnaic text by settling arguments it left unanswered. The rabbis found appropriate Torah verses to connect to and support ideas in Mishnaic passages; they also included nonlegal material like stories. Eventually it got to the point where all of this enlarged text had to be studied, too. It was called the *Gemara*, which means "completion." When the *Mishnah* and *Gemara* were published together, the title given the combined work was the Talmud.

Structure of the Talmud and Gemara

Since much of the *Gemara* is a commentary on the *Mishnah*, it makes sense that the organization of the *Gemara* follows that of the *Mishnah*. Like the *Mishnah*, the Talmud consists of six orders. However, the Talmud does not include a *gemara*, "teaching," on every single tractate of the *Mishnah*.

This is the first page of the first volume of the Talmud, Berachot. It deals with the evening reading of the Shema. The page is composed of (1) The Mishnah; (2) The Gemora; (3) The Commentary of Rashi; (4) The Tosaphot – Collected comments of descendants and pupils of Rashi, mainly devoted to discussion on Rashi's commentary; (5) Ein Mishpat – Cross references to the code of Maimonides and other early codes of talmudic law; (6) Rav Nissim Gaon – The commentary of Rabbi Nissim ben Ya'akov, eminent eleventh-century scholar; (7) Gilyon Hashas – Footnotes to the text of Rabbi Akiva Eger (1761-1837), famous Posen rabbi; (8) Hagahot Habach – Marginal notes of Rabbi Yoel Sirkes (1561-1640). "Bach" is from the initials of his commentary on the codes BAyshit CHadas ("New House"); and (9) Mesoret Hashas – Cross references to other volumes of the Talmud.

A Page from the Talmud.

Reading the *Gemara* is like eavesdropping on the conversations of the *amoraim*, the rabbis who studied and interpreted the *Mishnah*. Imagine someone overhearing a conversation between you and your friends. You might begin talking about what happened in school, suddenly switch to talking about your weekend plans, jump to discussing your favorite music group, and then return to talk about what happened in

Reading the *Gemara*.

school. Someone overhearing you and your friends might not find it all that easy to follow.

In the same way, the *amoraim*, the rabbis of the *Gemara*, do not always stick strictly to the topic they start with. They begin with a *mishnah* and from there may go in many different directions. They may search for a biblical verse to support the law in the *mishnah*. They may tell a story to illustrate a point they want to make. They may end up talking about something completely different from what they started with. No matter where the rabbis go, their words convey their deep desire to understand the *mishnah* and teach it to others.

Shabbat Revisited

In the last chapter you examined a *mishnah* from Tractate *Shabbat*. In that *mishnah* you read the rabbis' explanation of types of work prohibited on Shabbat. Here is another *mishnah* from Tractate *Shabbat*, which mentions a different Shabbat prohibition. As you will see in the *gemara* that accompanies the *mishnah*, the rabbis of the *Gemara* felt that this *mishnah* required further explanation.

Mishnah

You may not hire laborers on the Sabbath or ask your neighbor to hire laborers for you.

(Tractate *Shabbat* 23:3)

Gemara

But is an action consisting of mere speech forbidden on the Sabbath? R. Hisda and R. Hamenuna both said that one may figure the accounts involving religion on the Sabbath. And R. Eleazar said: One may fix grants for charity to the poor on the Sabbath; and R. Jacob b. Idi said in the name of R. Yochanan: One may attend to matters involving the saving of life or the public welfare on the Sabbath and one may go to the synagogue to attend to communal affairs on the Sabbath; and R. Samuel b. Nahmani said in the name of R. Yochanan: One may go to the theater, the circus, or the basilicas [where one met with Roman officials] to attend to communal affairs on the Sabbath; and the school of Menashe taught: One may make arrangements for a child's betrothal on the Sabbath, or for a child's education or to teach him a trade. [All of these involve speech.] [The answer is]: The verse specifies that on the Sabbath you are not "to pursue your own business or speak ordinary speech" (Isaiah 58:13)—one's own business may not be transacted on the Sabbath, but one may transact heavenly affairs [one is under a religious commitment to attend to all matters listed above and they are therefore permissible on the Sabbath].

(Tractate *Shabbat* 150a)

| **ACTIVITIES** |

Which of these statements describe the structure of this *gemara*?
Check as many as you want:

_____ states the question it has about the *mishnah* passage

_____ gives the name of each rabbi whose opinion is quoted

_____ clearly states how each opinion quoted is connected to the opening question

_____ includes a biblical quote from Isaiah to support its answer

How well do you understand this *gemara*? In order to clarify the points of the *gemara* fill in the chart below.

Prohibition Stated in the Mishnah	Question the Gemara Asks	List of Activities Permitted by the Gemara	Answer the Gemara Gives to Its Opening Question

Based on your understanding of the *gemara* from Tractate *Shabbat* 150a, check the best answer to the question "Is an action consisting of mere speech forbidden on the Sabbath?"

_____ No. It is not forbidden because so many other activities involving speech are permitted on the Sabbath.

_____ Yes. It is forbidden when the matter being spoken about involves your personal business matters such as hiring workers.

Women and Reading from the Torah

Sometimes the *gemara* raises as many questions as it answers and requires further explanation by later rabbis. An example of this is the following *gemara* on one of the greatest honors given during Jewish services, *aliyah latorah*. *Aliyah latorah* involves being called "to go up to the Torah" to read, or more often to chant, the blessings over the Torah and then look on while a reader recites aloud from the Torah scroll. Until a few decades ago, this honor was given only to men. Today, in all Reform and Reconstructionist congregations and in many Conservative congregations, both men and women may receive this honor. Read the following *gemara*, which discusses this matter.

Our rabbis taught: All are qualified to be among the seven [who are called up to read the Torah or recite the blessings over the Torah], even a minor [someone under bar mitzvah age] and a woman, but the sages said that a woman should not read from the Torah out of respect for the congregation [*kevod hatzibur*].

(Tractate *Megillah* 23a)

This *gemara* suggests that qualified women could be given *aliyot latorah*, but it says they should not "out of respect for the congregation" *(kevod hatzibur)*. The problem is that the *gemara* does not clearly define *kevod hatzibur*. Commentators on this *gemara* also have not given a precise definition for this term. However, a former chief rabbi of Israel, Ben Zion Uziel, states that *kevod hatzibur* means that if women are given *aliyot latorah* it will appear that there are no men in the congregation who know how to perform this task. In other words, giving women *aliyot* might show up the men and cause them to be embarrassed.

ACTIVITY

What do you think? Write a letter to Ben Zion Uziel, stating your opinion on whether or not women should receive *aliyot latorah* and what you think of Rabbi Uziel's definition of *kevod hatzibur*.

Dear Rabbi Uziel,

_____

_____

_____

_____

The Importance of Education

While we have talked about the *Mishnah* and the *Gemara* as guidebooks for living a Jewish life, it is important to note that not every idea is presented in a legal or halachic form. There is a great deal of nonlegal material in the *Gemara*, which presents important ideas through a rich story format known as *aggadah*.

The rabbis placed a great deal of importance on studying and learning. They believed that a person could move closer to God through study. With this goal in mind they established schools for studying Torah and other sacred texts. In the beginning these schools charged fees for each lecture. Many students struggled to make enough money to attend these classes. In the Babylonian Talmud we find a moving story about one student's burning desire to study.

Hillel the Elder was poor and needy. He spent half of his daily earnings to attend the lectures in the school of Shemaiah and Avtalyon. One winter day he was out of work. He had no money, and the doorkeeper would not let him into the house of study. But Hillel was determined not to miss the lesson. He climbed up to the roof and listened to the discussion through the skylight. Heavy snow began to fall and covered him. But he was concentrating so intently on the lecture that he did not notice. When evening came, he could not move because of the cold; so he lay there all night long. On the following morning the study hall was darker than usual. The students looked up and were astonished to see a human figure lying across the skylight. They rushed to the roof and carried a nearly frozen Hillel down and into the classroom. They placed him by a fire and revived him. From that day on Hillel was given permission to enter the house of study without charge.

(Tractate *Yoma* 35b)

ACTIVITIES

Which of the following words would you use to describe Hillel?

___ committed   ___ crazy   ___ stubborn   ___ hungry for knowledge

___ persistent   ___ cheap   ___ foolish   ___ clever

Why do you think this story is included in the Talmud?

_____ to illustrate the importance of study to the rabbis

_____ to describe the character of Hillel

_____ to discuss the question of charging fees for lectures

_____ to describe the harsh weather conditions

Based on this *aggadah* (nonlegal Talmud selection), what type of work do you think Hillel did as an adult? Be prepared to explain your choice.

_____ a baker   _____ a gardener   _____ a diamond merchant

_____ a rabbi   _____ a carpenter   _____ a banker

Praising God

Leah, one of our four matriarchs, was the first wife of Jacob. When God saw that Jacob liked his second wife, Rachel, more than he liked Leah, God lifted Leah's spirits by giving her many children: the first was Reuben, the second Simeon, the third Levi, and the fourth Judah. When Judah was born, she declared, "This time I will praise *Adonai*." (*Bereshit* 29:35) The rabbis of the Talmud interpret Leah's remark this way.

There was no one that praised the Holy One, blessed be *Adonai*, until Leah came and praised *Adonai*. . . . The rabbis go on to explain that Leah's words, "This time . . .," mean that up until this moment no one else had directly and intentionally praised God.

(Tractate *Berachot* 7b)

ACTIVITIES

Which of the following do you think best explains the purpose behind this talmudic comment?

_____   1. I think that this comment means that the rabbis wanted to emphasize the greatness of women.

_____   2. I think that this comment means that the rabbis wanted to emphasize the greatness of the matriarchs.

_____   3. I think that this comment means that the rabbis wanted to explain the practice of praising God.

_____   4. I don't agree with any of the above. I think that the rabbis' point is

_____

ACTIVITIES (CONTINUED)

Think of a time when you wanted to praise God. Write your own thanks to God.

_____

_____

_____

_____

_____

CHAPTER

10 Summary

In this chapter you began to see how the *Gemara* builds on and expands the teachings of the *Mishnah*. From these selections you witnessed firsthand that the *Gemara* covers a wide range of topics. Sometimes the *Gemara* focuses on halachic or legal concerns like working on Shabbat or who is permitted to read from the Torah. Other times the *Gemara* uses nonlegal writings called *aggadah to* teach us values like the importance of study and living by good moral standards. You even discovered that in some passages the *Gemara* is not totally clear and requires further comment and interpretation.

In the next chapter you will be formally introduced to a collection of rabbinic writings called *Midrash*. *Midrashim* are often thought of as stories, but, as you will learn, they are much more. You may even be surprised to find out that you have already written a *midrash* without even knowing it.

Ark of the Covenant Brought to Jerusalem. *J. Stradan (Stradanus), 1908-1909.*

Midrash *is a method of interpreting the Torah. People also interpret the Torah through artwork. The same biblical scene may often be depicted in different ways by different artists. Compare the above illustration of King David entering Jerusalem with illustrations showing the same scene on pages 61 and 77 of this book.*

How does each illustration tell us something new or different about the biblical episode?

11 MIDRASH

About This Chapter: *Midrash* is yet another part of rabbinic literature that was originally transmitted orally. It is best known in its story form although many *midrashim* also deal with matters of Jewish law. In this chapter you will discover how and why *midrashim* were created, study a few *midrashim*, and then try your hand at writing your own.

Midrash as Interpretation

Midrash is a *process* of interpretation, which searches for meaning and analyzes the message of verses from the Torah. *Midrash* is also the name given to the *end result*. *Midrash* is generally written in the form of a story. The rabbis who contributed to the creation of *midrashim* knew that stories are a powerful teaching tool, and they used stories well. However, the rabbis did not believe that they were just fabricating stories to make a point. For the rabbis, the lessons included in any *midrash* had their origins in the Torah. The rabbis who created *midrashim* believed that their task was to uncover the secret messages hidden in the words of the Bible. They saw themselves more as detectives than as authors.

As readers of the *midrashim*, we get to figure out what the messages are and how they are connected to Torah. We have to decide what is the question or questions that a *midrash* is asking. Then we try to figure out what answer is given by the *midrash*.

Types of Midrash

There is no single volume or organized collection of all midrashic writings. Unlike the *Mishnah* or the Talmud, there was no systematic approach to the creating and writing of *midrashim*. It is more accurate to call *midrash* a type of biblical interpretation by rabbis or scholars over hundreds of years. There are many books of *midrashim* that have been collected and organized. These collections are often grouped according to books of the Torah. *For example: Bereshit Rabbah* is a collection of *midrashim* on the Book of Genesis.

There are two main types of *midrash*. Some *midrashim* focus on matters of Jewish law and are known as *midrash halachah*. Others are more wide-ranging in content, more storylike, and less legal. These are known as *midrash aggadah*. In this chapter, you will examine examples of *midrash aggadah*.

The Goal of Midrash

Midrash, whether legal or nonlegal, seeks to make the Torah text clearer and easier to follow. It tries to fill in the gaps when it seems that parts are missing in the Torah narrative. It also works to clarify confusing parts in the text. Finally, *midrash* interprets the Bible in ways that keep it meaningful as the times change. *For example*: After the destruction of the Temple, people looked to the verses of Torah for consoling ideas and thoughts. Also, people needed guidance on how to behave since it was no longer possible to offer sacrifices to God. Many *midrashim* were created with these important needs in mind.

As the Dust of the Earth

Throughout this book we have discussed the importance of the *berit* between God and the Jewish people. As mentioned earlier, in *Bereshit*/Genesis, God first establishes the *berit* with our ancestors, Abraham, Isaac, and Jacob. In *Bereshit*/Genesis 13:16, God restates the *berit* with Abraham with the words, "I will make your offspring as the dust of the earth, so that if one can count the dust of the earth, then your offspring too can be counted." The following is a beautiful poetic *midrash* that elaborates on this Torah verse.

As the dust of the earth extends from one end of the world to the other,
So your children will be scattered from one end of the world to the other.
And as the dust of the earth can be blessed only through water,
So Israel too can be blessed only in virtue of the Torah, which is compared to water. . . .
And as dust is made to be trampled on,
So your children too will be made for kingdoms to trample on. . . .
And as dust wears vessels of metal away, but itself endures forever,
So with Israel: All the idolatrous nations shall disappear,
But Israel shall endure.

(*Bereshit Rabbah* 41:9)

Miriam's Well

The Bible tells us that Miriam, Moses' sister, was an important leader of the Jewish people. She watched over her baby brother as his basket floated down the river. She led everyone in singing and praising God after the crossing of the Sea of Reeds. To learn how she was rewarded for her actions, let us look at some biblical passages and then at a *midrash*.

Torah

1] . . . [The Children of Israel] encamped at Rephidim, and there was no water for the people to drink. **2]** The people quarreled with Moses. "Give us water to drink," they said; and Moses replied to them, "Why do you quarrel with me? Why do you try *Adonai*?" **3]** But the people thirsted there for water; and the people grumbled against Moses and said, "Why did you bring us up from Egypt, to kill us and our children and livestock with thirst?" **4]** Moses cried out to *Adonai*, saying, "What shall I do with this people? Before long they will be stoning me!" **5]** Then *Adonai* said to Moses, "Pass before the people; take with you some of the elders of Israel, and take along the rod with which you struck the Nile, and set out. **6]** I will be standing there before you on the rock at Horeb. Strike the rock and water will issue from it, and the people will drink." And Moses did so in the sight of the elders of Israel.

(*Shemot*/Exodus 17:1-6)

Miriam leads the Israelites as they sing and praise God after the crossing of the Sea of Reeds.

Midrash

The water that flowed for them on this spot served not only as a relief for their present need, but on this occasion there was revealed to them a well of water, which did not abandon them in all their forty years' wandering, but accompanied them on all their marches. God performed this great miracle for the merits of Miriam the prophet, and therefore it was known as "Miriam's Well."

(*Mechilta Va'yassa* 6:52; *Shemot Rabbah* 26:2)

Which of the questions below do you think is the question the *midrash* is answering? _____

1. How did the Children of Israel obtain water while they were in the desert?

2. Why did God make the water flow from the rock when the people were constantly complaining?

3. What was Miriam's reward for her good deeds?

_____

Do you think that this was a fitting reward? _____

How were Miriam's actions and the reward connected? _____

_____

_____

_____

King David

How should a leader act? Must a political leader always play the role of a head of state? In Chapter 6 of this book, *Nevi'im*/Prophets, we studied a passage from II Samuel 6:12-22. In it we find a description of King David's behavior on the day that he led the parade of people bringing the Ark of *Adonai* into Jerusalem.

14] David whirled with all his might before *Adonai*; David was girt with a linen *ephod*. 15] Thus David and all the House of Israel brought up the Ark of *Adonai* with shouts and with blasts of the horn.
16] As the Ark of *Adonai* entered the City of David, Michal daughter of Saul looked out of the window and saw King David leaping and whirling before *Adonai*; and she despised him for it.

(II Samuel 6:14-16)

So what is going on here? A king leaping and whirling? Is David forgetting his position? His wife, Michal, surely thinks so, and she bluntly tells David. But the next *midrash* draws very different conclusions about David's actions.

And David danced before *Adonai* with all his might; and David was girded with a linen *ephod*. (II Samuel 6:14) Come and see how much David humbled himself in honor of the Holy One, blessed be *Adonai*! David should have simply walked before the ark like a king, robed in his royal apparel. But no! He dressed himself in fairest garb in honor of the ark, and played before it . . . .

(*Bemidbar Rabbah* 4:20)

ACTIVITIES

What exactly are the conclusions of this *midrash*? Which of the following do you think best describes the position taken by the *midrash*?

_____ 1. David forgot his role as king, and that probably was not a good idea.

_____ 2. David did not let his kingship get in the way of rejoicing before God, who is, after all, the ultimate King.

_____ 3. The rabbis who wrote this *midrash* think that Michal is too strict in her opinion of how a king should behave.

_____ 4. David was devoted to God and Torah, as we see from his sincere excitement over these events that lead him to dance and rejoice openly.

What do *you* think? Was David out of line? Did he fail the people by acting out his true emotions? Or was his act a great example of humility before God? Describe your thoughts.

_____

_____

_____

Write Your Own Midrash

Now that you have read several examples of *midrashim*, it's time to try your hand at creating your own. The well-known story of Cain and Abel offers a natural place for a midrashic interpretation. This disturbing story tells of the first case of murder. What are the circumstances revolving around this crime? Let's look at the Torah verses from *Bereshit*/Genesis 4:1-8 that describe this incident.

Cain and Abel. *Cologne, 1470s?*

Torah

1] Now the man knew his wife Eve, and she conceived and bore Cain, saying, "I have gained a male child with the help of *Adonai.*" **2]** She then bore his brother Abel. Abel became a keeper of sheep, and Cain became a tiller of the soil. **3]** In the course of time, Cain brought an offering to *Adonai* from the fruit of the soil; **4]** and Abel, for his part, brought the choicest of the firstlings of his flock. *Adonai* paid heed to Abel and his offering, **5]** but to Cain and his offering God paid no heed. Cain was much distressed and his face fell. **6]** And *Adonai* said to Cain, "Why are you distressed,/And why is your face fallen?/ **7]** Surely, if you do right,/There is uplift./But if you do not do right/Sin couches at the door;/Its urge is toward you,/Yet you can be its master."

8] Cain said to his brother Abel . . . and when they were in the field, Cain set upon his brother Abel and killed him.

(*Bereshit* 4:1-8)

What happens here appears to be simple. But is it? Two brothers, one a shepherd and one a farmer, make offerings to God. God responds positively to the offering of the shepherd, Abel, but does not respond to the offering of the farmer, Cain. God notes Cain's disappointment and speaks to him. Then the brothers are in the field. They have some kind of discussion, and the next thing we know one of them kills the other. What? Murder prompted by the rejection of a sacrifice? Or was it something else? What did they discuss in the field? Did Abel somehow provoke his brother?

ACTIVITY

Write your own *midrash*. Fill in the missing dialogue between Cain and Abel in the field.

Cain: _____

Abel: _____

Cain: _____

Abel: _____

and when they were in the field, Cain set upon his brother Abel and killed him.

CHAPTER

11 Summary

Throughout your life you have probably heard many stories about the people and events of the Torah, and no doubt many of these were *midrashim*. Through this chapter you have gained a better appreciation of the workings of *midrashim*. You have looked at and studied several *midrashim*. You now clearly understand that *midrash aggadah* is a way of expanding on and enriching the words of the Torah.

This is the last chapter of this unit. Yet, the pursuit of Jewish knowledge and the compiling of Jewish books of learning did not end when the texts discussed in these chapters were completed. In the next unit of our book you will study writings from three of the best-known and respected teachers in Jewish history. You will glimpse into their worlds and sample their fascinating efforts to keep alive the tradition of Jewish study and Jewish life.

Rabbinic Writings from the Middle Ages to Today

About This Unit: It is truly amazing how long both the Torah and the Talmud have been around. They have been kept alive through the ongoing process of interpretation and expansion. In this unit you will be introduced to three of the greatest Jewish teachers of the Middle Ages and the ways they tried to make Jewish learning available to larger numbers of people. You will also learn about the ongoing tradition of responsa literature, in which rabbis answer questions about Jewish law.

"Turn It, Turn It"

In the Tractate *Pirke Avot*, "Sayings of the Fathers," of the *Mishnah* (5:25) we read: "Turn it [the Torah] and turn it again for everything is in it; and contemplate it and grow gray and old over it and stir not from it, for you can have no better guide than it." And so, teachers and students have poured over the pages of the Torah, turning it and turning it again, looking for new meanings, clearer explanations, and more meaningful interpretations. We know from previous reading in this book that the *Mishnah, Gemara,* and the Midrash are all responses to this order to "turn it and turn it again." And the turning and turning again did not end with the completion of these works. The period of Jewish history known as the Middle Ages (from approximately the early 600s C.E. to the second half of the 1600s C.E.) was a time of tremendous creativity in the world of Jewish learning. A continuous stream of dedicated and often brilliant scholars devoted their lives to exploring the world of Jewish texts. Their efforts helped keep Judaism in step with the changing needs and concerns of the times.

Three Rabbis Not to Miss

In the next three chapters you are going to meet three famous scholars who devoted their lives to the study of Torah. They shared their wisdom through their writings. These writings have made Jewish texts and Jewish living easier for generations and generations of Jews.

The first scholar is Rashi, born Shelomoh ben Isaac. He lived most of his life in France. His extensive commentaries open our eyes to the lessons of the Torah and the Talmud.

Next comes Maimonides, also called Rambam. He was born in Spain in 1135 and died in Egypt in 1204. He was a doctor as well as a rabbi and philosopher. Rambam is best known for his Jewish law code, the *Mishneh Torah*, and his philosophical work, the *Guide for the Perplexed*. Rambam wanted to make Jewish learning available to greater numbers of Jews, and he hoped that his writings would help achieve that goal.

The third scholar is Joseph Karo, also born in Spain but over three hundred years after Rambam. He eventually settled in Tsfat in the Land of Israel, where he became famous for his studies in the secrets of mysticism and for his neatly organized and easily readable code of Jewish law, the *Shulchan Aruch*. For centuries the *Shulchan Aruch* has served as *the* major reference resource on Jewish law.

The combined life spans of Rashi, Rambam, and Joseph Karo stretched over five hundred years. Yet, they shared a common commitment to Jewish learning and study. In the coming chapters you will explore some of their writings. You will also come to your own conclusions about why they remain so respected and important to this day.

12 The Torah Commentaries of Rashi

About This Chapter: Studying the Torah with the Rashi commentary is like having your own personal tutor. In this chapter you will get to study a few of Rashi's Torah commentaries. You will also find out the meaning of the word *peshat* and learn why Rashi is known as the greatest Jewish commentator of all time.

Martin Lemelman, painting

Rabbi Shelomoh ben Isaac, *known as Rashi (1040-1105).*

Rashi's World and His Work

In 1040 in Troyes, France, Shelomoh ben Isaac was born. We do not know many details about his early life, but we do know that he began his education in the city of Troyes, a busy trade center. After he married, he went to study in the great Jewish academies in Germany. His chapel, in Worms, Germany, still stands. At age twenty-five he returned to Troyes. There, like many Jews living in northern France during the 1000s, he made his living growing grapes. He lived at a time when the Jewish communities of France were close knit. Life in the communities revolved around work and observing and celebrating the events of Jewish life. Contact with the non-Jewish world was generally limited to business matters. Rashi's writings reflect the world he lived in. We may find an occasional French word thrown into his Hebrew commentaries, but his writings concentrate on rabbinic teachings and law and rarely mention things from the outside world.

A few years after his return to Troyes, Rashi established a school. As his status as a scholar and teacher rose, he obtained the title rabbi. He came to be known by the name **RaSHI**, a combination of the first letters of **R**abbi **Sh**elomoh ben **I**saac. In his school, Rashi continued his work, which he had begun in Germany, on commentaries of the *Tanach*. In his biblical commentaries, Rashi goes through the text verse by verse, offering explanations, commenting on grammatical structure, and emphasizing points of Jewish law. He is remarkable as a biblical commentator, one of the earliest to write this type of a verse-by-verse running Torah commentary. This format makes it fairly easy to go from a Torah verse to a commentary and back to the next Torah verse. Rashi also produced a very impressive, thorough commentary on the entire Talmud.

During his lifetime he was honored and respected as a great teacher. In fact, his Torah commentary was the first Hebrew book printed.* While he possessed great skill as an interpreter of sacred texts, he was willing to listen to the ideas of his students and to include them in his writings. Studying a text with the Rashi commentary is like having a teacher at your side. There are times when you wish he were around to clear up a point or two! Now it's time for you to study some of Rashi's Torah commentaries.

Torah Commentaries

From your study of the Torah excerpts in earlier chapters you learned that often there are many possible interpretations of a Torah verse. You read the ideas of important scholars, and you offered your own interpretations. Rashi used two basic approaches to interpreting the text: the *peshat* method, which explains a Torah verse in the most direct and straightforward way, and the *derash* method, which quotes *midrashim* and uses them to explain a Torah verse. Rashi is known as the "father of the French school of the *peshat* method" because he put greater emphasis on the *peshat* than other scholars of his time. While he also often quoted *midrashim* in his commentary in order to support his interpretation, he generally put greater stress on the *peshat* interpretation.

* *The Rashi commentary on the Torah, the first known Hebrew book to be printed, was printed alone without the text of the Torah. Also noteworthy about this book is that the printer chose a cursive Hebrew typeface. Almost all later publications of Rashi commentaries used the same typeface. Thus it came to be known as Rashi script. The letters are more curvy than other types of Hebrew print, and it takes a little practice to get used to reading them.*

Mikraot Gedolot (literally, "the Great Scriptures") is known in English as the rabbinic Bible.

Mikraot Gedolot presents the Hebrew text of the Torah surrounded by commentaries. Rashi's commentary is always included. The number of other commentaries depends on the size of the page. This page includes (1) The Torah – The passage shown is the beginning of the Book of Exodus; (2) Targum – A translation into Aramaic, traditionally attributed to Onkelos, a proselyte to Judaism, about the end of the first century; (3) Rashi's Commentary; (4) Ramban – The commentary of Rabbi Moshe ben Nachman (Nachmanides) (1194-1270), a Spanish talmudic scholar and physician; (5) ibn Ezra – Avraham ben Meir (1093-1167), a Spanish-born poet and commentator; (6) Commentary on ibn Ezra – This commentary by Rabbi Shlomo Zalman Netter was written to explain ibn Ezra's commentary; (7) Sforno – Obadia Sforno (1475-1550) was a physician who lived in Italy; (8) Rashban – Rabbi Shmuel ben Meir (1085-1174) lived in France; (9) Masorah – These are notes and rules on writing, spacing, and paragraphing of the Sefer Torah text; and (10) Toledot Aharon – This gives the talmudic reference wherever a biblical phrase or sentence is quoted in the Talmud.

121

Rashi was not content to merely explain some verses; he also incorporated Hebrew grammar lessons into his explanations of some verses. Rashi rarely mentioned the place in the Talmud or a *midrash* from which he got ideas, but, fortunately, over time scholars have searched for the sources and filled them in.

Rashi on the Spies

In an earlier chapter, we studied the story from *Bemidbar*/Numbers 13 about Moses sending spies to scout the Land of Israel before the Israelites entered it. The Torah describes Moses' instructions to the spies and what the spies saw on their mission. To refresh your memory the Torah verses are included below. They appear with Rashi's commentary. You will notice that Rashi's commentary goes in an orderly fashion from verse to verse. If Rashi had no comments on a particular verse, he moved on to the next.

Torah

17] When Moses sent them to scout the land of Canaan, he said to them,"Go up there into the Negeb and on into the hill country,

18] and see what kind of country it is. Are the people who dwell in it strong or weak, few or many?

19] Is the country in which they dwell good or bad? Are the towns they live in open or fortified?

20] Is the soil rich or poor? Is it wooded or not? And take pains to bring back some of the fruit of the land."
— Now it happened to be the

Rashi's Commentary

17] *Go up there into the Negeb.* It (the Negeb) was the worst part of the Land of Israel. Moses then told them to check out this area first because he was following the practice of a merchant who shows a perspective buyer the worst goods first and afterwards shows him the best.

18] *And see what kind of country it is.* There are countries that produce strong people, and there are countries that produce weak people; there are countries that produce a large population, and there are countries that produce a small population.

18] *Are the people who dwell in it strong or weak?* Moses gave the spies a clue as to how to interpret the strength of the people in the next phrase 19] *Are the towns they live in open or fortified?* which means: if they live in open cities they are strong, since they clearly rely on their own strength, but if they live in fortified cities [walled] they are weak.

19] *Is the country in which they dwell good or bad?* Does it have springs and other good and healthy supplies of water.

20] *Now it happened to be the season of the first ripe grapes.* The early stage of the days when the grapes were ripening.

season of the first ripe grapes.

21] They went up and scouted the land....

23] They reached the wadi Eshcol, and there they cut down a branch with a single cluster of grapes—it had to be borne on a carrying frame by two of them—and some pomegranates and figs. . . .

25] At the end of forty days they returned from scouting the land.

26] They went straight to Moses and Aaron and the whole Israelite community at Kadesh in the wilderness of Paran, and they made their report to them and to the whole community, as they showed them the fruit of the land.

27] This is what they told him: "We came to the land you sent us to; it does indeed flow with milk and honey, and this is its fruit.

28] However, the people who inhabit the country are powerful, and the cities are fortified and very large; moreover, we saw the Anakites there.

(*Bemidbar* 13:17-28)

23] *It had to be borne on a carrying frame by two of them.* What is meant by the statement "It had to be borne on a carrying frame by two of them," do I not know that it was *carried* "by two men"? Why then does it add the word two? It does not mean as you might think "by two men," but rather the two here refers to "upon two frames." How was that done? Eight of the spies carried the cluster of grapes. Besides these, one spy took the figs and one the pomegranate, but Joshua and Caleb did not carry anything [even though Moses had told them all to "bring back some of the fruit of the land." v.20]. Joshua and Caleb did not participate in the carrying because they knew that the main intent of the other spies was to bring back an evil report. They knew that the other spies would lie and say, "Just as the fruits of the land are extraordinary in size, so are the people extraordinary in size."

27] *We came to the land you sent us to; it does indeed flow with milk and honey.* They stated this because even though they intended to tell lies they had to strengthen their false report with some true facts.

Return of the Spies from the Land of Promise.

Gustave Doré, France, 1865

123

Rashi's comments are often answers to questions he has about a verse. However, he rarely states the question directly. Below is a list of questions answered in Rashi's commentary on *Bemidbar* 13:17-27. Next to each question write the number of the verse it goes with.

_____ Why, if the spies intended to give a false report of what they saw in the Land of Israel, did they begin with truthful information?

_____ How were the spies to know if the people were strong or weak?

_____ Since the Torah never includes unnecessary details, why does it include the word *two* in this verse?

_____ What does the text mean by a good or bad country?

_____ Why did Moses tell the spies to begin the mission in the Negeb?

Even though the sources for Rashi's comments are not included above, complete these two statements. (You may want to review the explanations of *peshat* and *derash* given earlier.)

I think that Rashi's comment on verse _____ is an example of the *peshat* method of commentary because _____

_____

I think that Rashi's comment on verse _____ is an example of the *derash* method of commentary because _____

_____

Rashi and the Death of Moses

In the last chapter of *Devarim*/Deuteronomy you read about the death of Moses. These dramatic verses raised questions for Rashi just as they did for you when you studied them before. The verses are again included here with the Rashi commentary.

Torah

5] So Moses the servant of *Adonai* died there, in the land of Moab, at the command of *Adonai*.

Rashi's Commentary

5] *So Moses the servant of* Adonai *died there.* Is it possible that Moses died and *then* wrote: "And Moses died there"? No, it is not possible; so the answer must be that Moses wrote everything in the Torah up to these verses, and Joshua wrote the rest. Rabbi Meir [a *tanna* of the second century C.E.] said: How is it possible that the Book of the Torah would be missing any verses?; for we read in an earlier verse, *before the account of Moses' death was written in the Torah*, that Moses told the Children of Israel, "Take this Book of the Torah and place it beside the Ark of the Covenant of *Adonai* your God, and let it remain there." (*Devarim* 31:26) So the answer, according to Rabbi Meir, is that the Holy One, blessed be God, dictated these verses, about the death of Moses, to Moses before he died, and Moses wrote them down with tears in his eyes.

5] *At the command of* Adonai. Command actually means "mouth," so that Moses died "at the command [mouth] of *Adonai*" means that Moses died by a kiss from God.

6] God buried Moses in the valley in the land of Moab, near Beth-peor; and no one knows his burial place to this day.

6] *God buried Moses.* That is, the Holy One, blessed be God, in God's glory, buried Moses.

7] Moses was a hundred and twenty years old when he died; his eyes were undimmed and his vigor unabated.

7] *His eyes were undimmed and his vigor unabated.* Even in death his eyes did not lose their spark of life, and decomposition had no effect on his body.

8] And the Israelites bewailed Moses in the steppes of Moab for thirty days.

The period of wailing and mourning for Moses came to an end.

9] Now Joshua son of Nun was filled with the spirit of wisdom because Moses had laid his hands upon him; and the Israelites heeded him, doing as *Adonai* had commanded Moses.

10] Never again did there arise in Israel a prophet like Moses—whom *Adonai* singled out, face to face,

10] *Never again did there arise in Israel a prophet like Moses—whom* Adonai *singled out face to face.* This means that Moses was familiar with God and used to speak to God at any time he desired, just as it is stated that Moses said, "And now I will ascent to *Adonai*." [Exodus 32:30]

11] for the various signs and portents that *Adonai* sent him to display in the land of Egypt, against Pharaoh and all his courtiers and his whole country,

12] and for all the great might and awesome power that Moses displayed before all Israel.

(*Devarim* 34:5-12)

12] *And for all the great might.* This refers to the fact that Moses received the Torah that was on the Tablets in his hands [for a *midrash* states that the Tablets were of extraordinary weight and a strong hand was required to hold them].

125

Match the question that Rashi is addressing with the correct number of the verse he is commenting on.

_____   What is an example of Moses' great might?

_____   Who buried Moses?

_____   Who wrote these verses about the death of Moses?

_____   How did death affect Moses?

_____   What was the cause of death?

_____   What was the nature of the relationship between God and Moses?

Never again did there arise in Israel a prophet like Moses—whom *Adonai* singled out, face to face. (34:10)

Write your own explanation of the meaning of these words. First write the question you have on the verse and then include your answer.

_____

_____

_____

_____

Summary

Rashi is considered the outstanding biblical and talmudic commentator of Jewish history. He gathered the ideas of others and then added comments and explanations of his own. After a little practice studying his commentaries, his style becomes easy to follow. This is because Rashi's goal was to explain the text in the most direct way. At times, he found it helpful to draw on a *midrash* for an explanation to place along with the simple meaning.

The influence of Rashi's commentaries crossed the boundaries of central Europe to include Jews everywhere. His works were widely circulated, especially after the introduction of printing in Europe. The translation of his Torah commentary into Latin, German, and English increased the numbers of people who could share in his wisdom. Rashi's legacy lives on and all who study Torah are indebted to him.

The Mishneh Torah of Rambam

About This Chapter: Rambam was one of the most remarkable Jews to ever live. He was not content to do things halfway. Therefore, his writings, like the *Mishneh Torah*, are both vast and thorough. In this chapter you will read Rambam's own reasons for writing the *Mishneh Torah*, and you will read excerpts that discuss matters that relate to your everyday life.

Rabbi Moses ben Maimon, *known as Rambam (1135-1204).*

From Moses to Moses

"From Moses to Moses there was none like Moses."
This quote sums up the reputation of Rabbi Moses ben

Maimon. It means that from the time of Moses of the Bible to the time of Moses ben Maimon there was no one who compared to Moses ben Maimon. He was born in 1135 C.E. in Cordoba, Spain. Like Rashi before him, as an adult he acquired the title rabbi and a name made up of a combination of the letters of his full name, **R**abbi **M**oses **B**en **M**aimon - **RaMBaM**.

When he was a teenager, Rambam and his family left Spain to escape the attacks of the Almohades, Moslems who had come to Spain from North Africa.* The family spent many years wandering around North Africa and the Land of Israel, then known as Palestine. Finally in 1165 they settled in Egypt. During the years of traveling around, Rambam kept up his studies so that by the time they settled in Egypt he was well on his way to becoming both a highly respected Jewish scholar and a doctor.

Rambam, who was also known by the Greek name Maimonides, possessed tremendous energy. He wrote works on Jewish law and philosophy. He maintained a very busy medical practice, a demanding writing schedule, and an active correspondence on public as well as private concerns. By age thirty-three he had published the first of his great works, a commentary on the *Mishnah*. The same year he was also appointed court physician for the royal court of Sultan Saladin, a position that required great medical knowledge and skill.

Twelve years later, in 1180, he published his extremely important Jewish law code, the *Mishneh Torah*. In this awesome work Rambam classified and organized all the laws of the Talmud into fourteen volumes. In addition to all this, Rambam served as the unofficial head of the Cairo Jewish community. His letters include descriptions of how his house was constantly filled with people waiting for his guidance on solving disagreements according to Jewish law. It is hard to imagine when he had time to rest.

Rambam devoted years to studying and writing philosophy. He read and studied the writings of many famous Greek philosophers. In his impressive, complex *Guide for the Perplexed* he set out to examine Judaism in relationship to the philosophy of the Greek thinker Aristotle. Originally, Rambam wrote the book in Arabic. He also answered letters from Jews all over the world who requested his help on deciding matters of Jewish law. We are fortunate to have so many of his writings to study and learn from today.

* The Almohades were a group of Moslem fanatics who came from North Africa to invade southern Spain. Their oppressive behavior toward non-Moslems was not the rule of the day. In fact, Rambam lived during the end of what has been called the "Golden Age" of Spanish Jewish history, a time when Jews lived in relative harmony with their Arab Moslem neighbors.

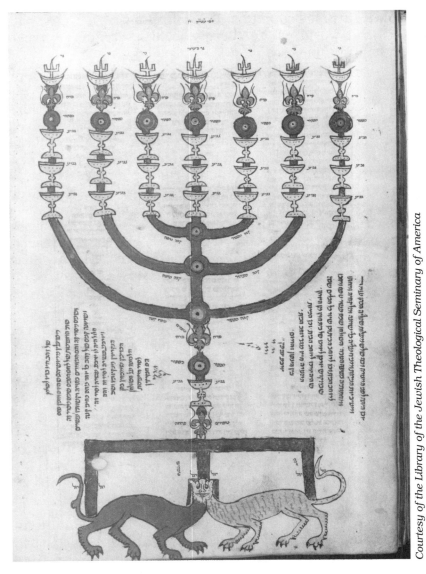

A Page from Rambam's *Mishneh Torah.*

The Mishneh Torah

Throughout his lifetime, Rambam lived in countries that were under Islamic rule. With the exception of fanatic groups like the Almohades, who caused his family and many others to flee southern Spain, Islamic rulers were relatively tolerant of their Jewish subjects. There was even a certain amount of contact between Jews and Moslems, the followers of Islam. This contact resulted in a sharing of literary styles, artistic ideas, and architectural techniques. The clear, direct, and orderly structure of Rambam's code of Jewish law reflects the influence of the Moslem world in which it was written. This contrasts with Rashi's writings, which were written in a world where there was little contact between Jews and non-Jews.

It took Rambam a decade to write his code of Jewish law, the *Mishneh Torah*. In the introduction to this fourteen-volume work, Rambam reviews the development of Jewish law from the time when Moses received the Torah at Mount Sinai to his own time. Rambam points out the steady decline in Torah study that had occurred over the generations. He explains his hope to end this decline by writing this code of Jewish law "so that the entire Oral Law might become systematically known to all." He further explains, "I entitled this work *Mishneh Torah* ['Repetition of the Law'] for the reason that a person who first reads the Written Law [the Torah] and then my fourteen volumes will know from it the whole of the Oral Law, without having occasion to consult any other book between them."

Rambam wrote in a concise manner, omitting all of the side conversations of earlier codes. Most amazing is the amount of material in the *Mishneh Torah*. Rambam addressed every aspect of *halachah* ("Jewish law"). He covers everything from the basic principles of Jewish belief to laws no longer practiced, such as rules regarding Temple sacrifices. Now that you have a general idea about the characteristics of the *Mishneh Torah*, it is time to study some selections.

Tzedakah

Ever since you were a small child you have been taught about the importance of helping others. You learned that the Hebrew term for giving money to those in need is *tzedakah*. And no doubt you have contributed to a variety of funds to help others in your community and Jews around the world. There are many different ways of giving *tzedakah*. Is one way better than others? Is it better for the giving to be direct, or should someone act as a go-between? What is the best attitude for the giver to have? In Book Seven–Seeds, under "Gifts to the Poor," Rambam describes eight degrees of giving *tzedakah*, from the lowest to the highest levels.

The eight degrees are listed below but not in order. Read through them and then put them in order. Number eight should be the one you think is the highest level of *tzedakah*, and number seven the second highest, and so on.

_____ Giving less than you should but giving graciously.

_____ Giving grudgingly, reluctantly, or with regret.

_____ Giving before you are asked to give.

_____ Giving without knowing to whom you are giving although the receiver knows that you are the giver.

_____ Giving anonymously (without making your identity known).

_____ Giving what you should but only after you are asked.

_____ Giving without knowing to whom you are giving and without the receiver knowing from whom the help is coming.

_____ Giving a gift, a loan, or help in finding a job so that the receiver will become self sufficient and no longer in need of *tzedakah*.

Which level of *tzedakah* is described in the following scenarios?

1. Your class is scheduled to go on a field trip. Everyone is required to pay $10. Your friend does not have the money. You take up a collection among your classmates, telling them it's to help someone go on the trip, without identifying the person. You then give the money to the teacher, asking her to tell your friend that money has been donated to cover the fee.

   Giving _____

2. For your bat mitzvah you receive gifts of money. You decide to give some to a *tzedakah* project that helps newly arrived Soviet Jews in your community. You give the money to a local organization, and they distribute the money to families in need.

   Giving _____

3. A terrible fire destroys the homes of a number of students in your school. The Parent-Teacher Organization establishes a collection of clothing for the families of these students. Your mom goes through your closet and takes out several of your favorite shirts to give away. They are really too small for you to wear, but you are angry that she has put them in the bag for the fire victims. It is your job to take the clothes to a collection spot at school. Your mother has to remind you three days in a row to take the clothes before you actually follow through and bring them.

   Giving _____

Reciting the Shema

Rambam wrote the *Mishneh Torah* with the hope that "the entire Oral Law might become systematically known to all." Part of his approach was to summarize materials found in the longer and more complex *Mishnah* and Talmud. To illustrate this point, below is a selection from Book Two of the *Mishneh Torah*. It is a summary of the beginning of Tractate *Berachot* of the *Mishnah*. The topic is the appropriate time to recite the *Shema*. From the Torah, *Devarim* 6:7, we learn that we are commanded to recite the *Shema* twice daily. But when exactly are the right times? Read on to find out Rambam's answer, as presented in Book Two–Adoration.

The *Shema* is read twice every day — in the evening and in the morning, as it is said, "and when you lie down and when you rise up" (*Devarim* 6:7), the phrases in this text meaning at the time when people are lying down, that is, at night, and at the same time when they have risen, that is, by day.

ACTIVITY

Using the *Mishneh Torah* selection as your guide, answer the following letters sent to the great rabbi Rambam.

My most esteemed Rambam,

I am not clear about exactly when I should recite the *Shema*. I have recently been ill and have to take frequent naps. Does this mean that I should say the *Shema* every time I lie down for a nap and every time I get up from my nap? I appreciate your help with this important matter.

Your humble questioner,
Solomon

Dear Solomon,

_____

_____

_____

Yours,
Rambam

Dear Rambam,

I have a question regarding when I am required to recite the *Shema*. I work from 11 P.M. to 7 A.M. This means that I *rise* to go to work at *night* and *lie down* to sleep in the *morning*. I am confused about what to do. Thank you so much for your help.

Your humble questioner,
Miriam

Dear Miriam,

_____

_____

_____

Yours,
Rambam

Students and Teachers

Since studying and learning are so important in Jewish tradition, it is not surprising to find that there are many laws regarding the relationships between students and teachers. These laws are found in the *Mishneh Torah*, Book One–Knowledge, under "Laws concerning the Study of Torah."

As students are bound to honor their teacher, so a teacher ought to show courtesy and friendliness to his students. The rabbis said, "Let the honor of your followers be as dear to you as your own honor." [*Mishnah*, Sayings of the Fathers 4:15] A person should take an interest in his pupils and love them, for they are his spiritual children who will bring him happiness in this world and in the world hereafter.

List five ways that a teacher can show respect for a student.

1. _____
2. _____
3. _____
4. _____
5. _____

List five ways that a student can bring happiness to a teacher.

1. _____
2. _____
3. _____
4. _____
5. _____

Deceiving People

Jewish law covers all aspects of life. There is no line dividing what we would call religious behavior (like celebrating holidays and performing rituals) and what we would call everyday activities (like business dealings and relations with neighbors). Everything you do can be a part of striving to be a good, moral, holy person. In Chapter 9, you read a *mishnah* about fairness in business. Rambam also devotes a large section of the *Mishneh Torah* to the laws concerning fair business practices. The following selection comes from Book Twelve–Acquisitions, under "Sales."

It is forbidden to deceive people in buying and selling or to deceive them by creating a false impression. A non-Jew and a Jew are to be treated alike in this respect. If one knows that an article he is selling has a defect, he must inform the buyer about it. It is forbidden to deceive people even by words.

Which of the following scenarios describe business practices that follow the laws in the above paragraph? Check the one(s) that fit.

_____ 1. An owner of a designer jeans outlet store gets in a new shipment of slightly imperfect women's jeans. He sees that the imperfections are so small that shoppers will not notice them. He considers selling them at a higher price along with the other jeans but decides to sell them at a reduced price, placing them on a special rack marked "Imperfect."

_____ 2. Mr. Stewart comes into a wine store. He looks over the kosher wines, trying to decide which to bring to his friend's house for a Passover seder. Mr. Shapiro, the owner of the store, asks if he needs some help. Mr. Stewart explains that as a non-Jew he has no idea about the differences between kosher wines. Mr. Shapiro sees that Mr. Stewart is holding two bottles, one twice as expensive as the other. He could say that the more expensive wine is much better, but in fact he really thinks that they taste about the same. He advises his customer to take the less expensive bottle.

_____ 3. You got a new bicycle for your birthday and decide to sell the old one. You carefully clean up the old bike. You repaint the body, change the tires, and put on a new seat. Then you put an ad in the paper, which says "Brand New Bicycle for Sale."

_____ 4. Your aunt is having a yard sale. She asks you to help her out. Her only instruction to you is, "Don't point out any defects. If the buyers don't see it, that's fine." So when a lady comes up to buy the old VCR and asks you if it works, you hesitate. Finally you answer, "Yes, it plays video tapes, but it does not record."

CHAPTER

13 | Summary

In this chapter you have studied a small portion of Rambam's code of Jewish law, the *Mishneh Torah*. You have been reminded through the excerpts and activities that Jewish law covers every aspect of life. And, while you did not get to explore some of Rambam's other works, like the *Guide for the Perplexed*, you have seen his exceptional skills as a master of organization and clear writing.

Even though Rambam failed to fulfill his goal of making his *Mishneh Torah* the sole reference for the sources of Jewish law, he, nonetheless, made a major contribution to the clarification of Jewish laws and ideas. Proof of this fact is the enduring attention and respect given to Rambam's works. Like the writings of Rashi, Rambam's texts continue to be read widely and studied today. In the next chapter, you will encounter another outstanding Jew of the Middle Ages, Joseph Karo, and learn about his efforts towards further codifying Jewish law.

Joseph Karo *(1488-1575) in the city of Tsfat, speaking to his students.*

14 The Shulchan Aruch of Joseph Karo

About This Chapter: Joseph Karo wrote the most widely used code of Jewish law, the *Shulchan Aruch*. In this chapter you will learn why he undertook this task. Also, you will explore the reasons for its tremendous popularity and examine a few samples from its pages.

Why Another Code?

Most North American school children know about the famous travels of Columbus from the poem that includes the line "In 1492 Columbus sailed the ocean blue." But 1492 is also important in Jewish history. In that year the Jews of Spain were cruelly expelled from their country. Joseph Karo was only four years old when he and his family were forced to leave Spain. Many of the expelled Jews went to neighboring Portugal, only to face expulsion from there a few years later. Others went north to Amsterdam. And some, like the Karo family, traveled around for years before settling into new permanent surroundings. In 1525 Karo finally settled in the beautiful city of Tsfat in the Land of Israel.

As his family traveled from one Jewish community to another, Karo learned that Jews did not observe Jewish law, *halachah,* in the same ways. He also realized that there were fewer and fewer truly learned Jewish scholars spread among the communities. This meant that, when questions of Jewish law arose, often there was no one with enough knowledge to answer the questions accurately and to serve as a guide for the people.

Karo decided to solve this problem by creating a standardized code of Jewish law. His goal was similar to Rambam's goal.* He wanted to codify (make a code of) Jewish law so that someone looking up a specific law could find it easily without having to search through the complexities of the Talmud. Karo began by methodically reading all the halachic writings available. He then set out to write a code in which he analyzed the many opinions on a given topic and concluded by giving a decision on what the law should be. This incredible task took over twenty years to complete,

* *Joseph Karo wanted to cover all aspects of Jewish law that touched the daily lives of Jews of his time. Therefore, unlike Rambam, he left out all laws that were no longer practiced (like laws connected to the Temple). However, he did follow Rambam's example by omitting all references to the sources from which he took his information.*

שולחן ערוך

מטור יורה דעה הנקרא בית יוסף

חברו הגאון מופת הדור החכם השלם מהרר יוסף קארו נרו בן מהרר אפרים קארו
זצל אשר אור תורתו זורחת כאור היום בעיר צפת תוב ב ומעיני תורתו נפוצות
ביהודה ובישראל נודע שמו: וחבר הספר הזה קיצור מחיבורו הגדול
אשר עשה על הארבעה טורים אשר קראם בית יוסף אשר
בם כח מעשיו הגיד וכל יקר ראתה עינו כדי שכל
מבקש ה'ימצא מבוקשו בנקל כל דין ודין על
מתכונתו באין אומר ואין דברים והכן
לכל מטה ושלחן וכסא ומנורה
אשר לאורו ילכו בטח: כי כן משנת רבי יוסף קב ונקי

ותהי ראשית מלאכתו זאת נגמן שכלה לפק פה ווניציאה הטורים :

The Title Page from the *Shulchan Aruch, 1564 edition.*

and the result was the code known as the *Bet Yosef.*
Unfortunately, the *Bet Yosef* proved to be too complex
for most Jews of Karo's time. So, in his old age, Karo
wrote a shortened code called the *Shulchan Aruch.*
Shulchan Aruch means "set table." It was Karo's intention to lay everything out in a neat and orderly manner
like a table set for a meal. In this concisely written
code, he leaves out the intricate arguments and analy-
sis found in the *Bet Yosef.* What remains is a well organized four-part code of Jewish law in which the laws
are stated directly with absolute authority and without

question. The four sections include every aspect of Jewish law still practiced in Karo's time. The code divides Jewish law into four categories: *Orah Hayim* ("Path of Life") on liturgical laws having to do with prayer; *Yoreh Deah* ("Teacher of Knowledge") on ritual laws; *Even Haezer* ("The Stone of Help") on marriage laws; and *Hoshen Hamispat* ("The Breastplate of Judgment") on civil laws.

Karo also pursued other areas of Jewish studies. The city of Tsfat, where he lived, was the home of many scholars who explored the world of Jewish mysticism. This area of study dealt with intense spiritual matters. Only those who had already mastered Jewish law were allowed to indulge in the study of this mysterious subject. Despite Karo's involvement in mysticism, his most enduring contribution to Jewish life was his code, the *Shulchan Aruch*. Thanks to the introduction of the printing press, the *Shulchan Aruch* was widely distributed to Jews living everywhere. It has had a lasting influence on the study of Jewish law. To this day it remains the most frequently used code of Jewish law.

The Mapa

Despite the incredibly thorough job done by Karo in the *Shulchan Aruch*, he fell short of his goal of writing *the* authoritative, universal code of Jewish law. The problem was that Karo's code reflected the customs and rabbinic decisions of only his own Sephardic background. For the *Shulchan Aruch* to appeal to Ashkenazic Jews, it needed a commentary that included the distinctive customs of Ashkenazic Jews.* The task of writing this commentary was undertaken by the Polish rabbi Moses Isserles (1520-1572). Isserles named his commentary the *Mapa*, which means "tablecloth." The completed combined efforts resulted in Isserles spreading his Ashkenazic "tablecloth" over Karo's "set table."

The Influence and Status of the Shulchan Aruch

Karo and Isserles lived during a time when Jews were being expelled from country after country. Jewish communities formed and disbanded. There was a great need for an easy-to-use authoritative list of do's and don'ts of Jewish law. The *Shulchan Aruch*, along with the *Mapa* commentary, filled this need. Also, the timing of the publication of the *Shulchan Aruch* helped its rapid spread and popularity. Since the *Shulchan Aruch*

* *Central and Eastern Europe came to be known by the Hebrew term* Ashkenaz. *Jews who come from these areas or whose roots begin there are called* Ashkenazim. *Jews whose roots go back to Spain or North Africa are called* Sephardim, *which comes from the Hebrew word for Spain,* Sepharad. *The basic Jewish beliefs and practices of the two groups are the same. They differ only in certain areas of customs and traditions.*

was the first code of Jewish law written after the invention of the printing press, more people were able to get a copy of it and read it than any other Jewish code written before. The contents of the *Shulchan Aruch* cover everything from A to Z in Jewish life, as you will see in the sample selections that follow.

Visiting the Sick

Did you know that Jewish law *commands* us to visit the sick? *Bikur Cholim* is the Hebrew term for this *mitzvah*. The specifics of how to carry out the *mitzvah* of visiting the sick are found in the *Shulchan Aruch* in *Yoreh Deah*. A few sample paragraphs follow. *Mapa* comments on the *Shulchan Aruch* are also included.

Shulchan Aruch

It is a religious duty to visit the sick. Relatives and friends may enter at once and strangers after three days. If the sickness [suddenly] overtakes the person, both relatives and friends and strangers may enter at once.

Even a prominent person must visit a humble one; even many times a day and even if the visitor is the same age as the sick person. One who increases [visits to the sick] is considered praiseworthy, provided one does not trouble the sick person.

Mapa

Some say that an enemy may visit a sick person. However, this does not seem plausible to me; one should not visit a sick person nor comfort a mourner whom one hates, since such a visit might lead [the sick person or the mourner] to think that the visitor is rejoicing in the misfortune and cause the sick person or mourner to feel depressed by the visit. This seems to me [to be the correct view].

ACTIVITIES

Why do you think relatives and friends are allowed to visit a sick person before other less familiar visitors are allowed? _____

_____

_____

What do *you* think? Should an enemy be allowed to visit a sick person or someone in mourning? _____

Explain your answer. _____

_____

Laws of Mourning

How are you to act when someone near and dear to you dies? What are the laws relating to someone who is mourning the loss of a close relative? Just as there are many *mitzvot* about *Bikur Cholim*, "visiting the sick," there are quite a number of *mitzvot* that guide us when we comfort mourners or are in mourning ourselves.* These can be found in the *Shulchan Aruch*, in *Yoreh Deah*.

⁎ The seven days immediately following a funeral are known by the Hebrew term Shivah. *During this time people in mourning do not leave their homes except on Shabbat. Relatives and friends visit mourners and offer them support and comfort.*

Shulchan Aruch

The comforters are not permitted to begin [conversation] until the mourner begins first; . . . and as soon as the mourner nods the head in such a way that tells the comforters to go, the comforters must leave [so that the mourner may rest].

Throughout the seven days [of mourning] a mourner is forbidden to read the *Tanach* [Torah, the Prophets, and the Writings] [or to study] *Mishnah, Gemara, halachot,* or *aggadot.* If, however, the public needs the mourner to teach them, the mourner is permitted [to study and thus prepare for the lecture], provided that [during the presentation of the lecture] the mourner does not place [next to the mourner] an interpreter, rather the mourner should lecture [first] to another person, who, in turn, [conveys the lecture] to the interpreter, and the latter gives the lecture to the public.

Mapa

Or the mourner may give the lecture [directly to the public]. A mourner who is a scholar may give answers to questions of *halachah,* Jewish law, from an individual inquirer, provided the mourner is the only one available [to answer such questions] and the public needs the mourner. But a mourner is forbidden to lecture on *halachah* to students. Thus is the common practice, although some are lenient [in this matter].

ACTIVITY

Which of the following is the best explanation for the *mitzvah* that says a comforter has to wait for a mourner to speak first? Circle your choice.

1. This is to avoid the possibility of the comforter saying something stupid.

2. This is to let the mourner set the tone of the conversation.

3. This is because comforters are not always sure of the most comforting things to say.

The seven days of mourning (some Jews observe three instead of seven) are a way of showing respect for the dead and a time for the mourner to focus attention on the loss of a special person. The *Shulchan Aruch* and the *Mapa* differ on what is appropriate for a mourner to do in the case where the mourner's expertise may be needed by the community.

ACTIVITY

Imagine that you live in a small town where you are the *only* doctor, dentist, lawyer, or plumber. You are observing the days of mourning for the loss of someone close to you. Your services are needed. What do you do?

_____

_____

_____

_____

_____

Table Manners

Even if you were not aware of the specific *mitzvot* on visiting the sick and comforting mourners, you probably were not surprised to learn that they existed. But what about such everyday matters as table manners? Yes, those little habits that your parents constantly are correcting for you are also covered in this code of Jewish law. The *Shulchan Aruch* includes *mitzvot* on proper table manners in the volume entitled *Orah Hayim*. To see what the *Shulchan Aruch* has to say on this topic, read the following selections.

Shulchan Aruch

One should not drink the contents of a glass all at once, and if one does drink them all at once one is labeled a gobbler. Drinking the contents in two mouthfuls is well-mannered, but if one drinks the contents in three mouthfuls one is labeled as snobbish.

Mapa

However, it is permitted to drink the contents of a very small glass all at once . . . and, likewise, the contents of a very large glass may be drunk in three or four mouthfuls.

Shulchan Aruch

...One should not bite off a piece of bread and put the remainder back on the table.

...When one enters a house one should not say, "Give me something to eat," but should wait until the hosts offer food.

Mapa

A person should not say to a companion, "Come and partake of my hospitality in the same way that I partook of your hospitality." The reason is that this might look like repaying a debt and as if the first person were lending the second food. This could then result in a situation where, if the second feeds the first more that the first fed the second, it could look like the second one is repaying the debt with interest [and there are prohibitions against charging and paying interest]. However, it is permitted to say to one's companion, "Come and partake of my hospitality and I will partake of your hospitality some other time," and then one is permitted to eat even a larger meal from his hospitality.

ACTIVITY

Which of the following statements do you think best explains why Jewish law includes *mitzvot* about table manners and behavior connected to eating?

1. In every aspect of life we can work to live in ways that make us holier, more moral people.

2. The eating table is considered to be modeled after the Temple altar where sacrifices were offered to God.

Complete: I think _____ is the better answer because _____

_____

Special Blessings

We often go through our lives focusing on everyday details like school and work but rarely stop to appreciate all the wonders of nature around us. The *Shulchan Aruch* reminds us in *Orah Hayim* to take note of the beauty and power of our physical surroundings.

Shulchan Aruch

One should make a blessing over meteors (kinds of stars that shoot like an arrow across the length of the heavens from place to place and give a light that stretches out like a rod), earthquakes, and lightning flashes. In each of these cases one should say the blessing: *Baruch Atah Adonai Elohenu Melech ha'olam oseh ma'aseh vereshit.* "Blessed are You *Adonai* our God, Sovereign of the universe, who performs the work of creation." If one wishes, one may say the blessing: *Baruch Atah Adonai Elohenu Melech ha'olam shekocho ugevurato malei olam.* "Blessed are You *Adonai* our God, Sovereign of the universe, whose power and might fill the universe."

If one sees a rainbow, one should say the blessing: *Baruch Atah Adonai Elohenu Melech ha'olam zocher haberit vene'eman bivrito vekayam bema'amaro.* "Blessed are You *Adonai* our God, Sovereign of the universe, who remembers the covenant and is faithful to the covenant and true to the word."☆

☆ *When was the first time God made a rainbow to serve as a reminder of a covenant? (Hint: See Bereshit 9:12-13.)*

ACTIVITIES

Of the blessings given for experiencing various natural wonders, which would you choose to say? Fill in the chart below.

Natural Wonder	Performs the Work of Creation	Whose Power and Might Fill the Universe
shooting stars earthquakes lightning flashes		

Choose one of the natural wonders listed above and write your own blessing.

_____

_____

_____

_____

_____

As with Rashi and Rambam, there is much more to study of Karo's writings than we have studied in this chapter. Among his other works were important commentaries on the *Mishnah* and on the writings of Rashi, as well as his mystical writings mentioned earlier. However, we have justly focused on his most famous and influential work, the *Shulchan Aruch*. The *Shulchan Aruch* remains the last great code of Jewish law to be written. To this day, if someone wants to look up a specific Jewish law that is still in practice, the most common place to turn is to the *Shulchan Aruch*.

The writing of Jewish codes, a process that began with the *Mishnah*, was followed by the Talmud and several other codes, including Rambam's *Mishneh Torah*, and ended with Joseph Karo's *Shulchan Aruch*. However, the process of examining, interpreting, and expanding on Jewish law did not end. The tradition of rabbinic authorities receiving questions on Jewish law and writing responses, known as responsa, lives on to the present. In the next and final chapter of this text you will be introduced to examples of responsa. Be prepared for more surprises like the ones you found in this chapter.

15 Responsa: Our Changing Tradition

About This Chapter: Jewish law is a living law. Throughout the ages, we have interpreted, expanded, and shaped Torah to address the needs of changing times. We often have turned to rabbis and scholars with our questions and they have written carefully researched responses. Samples from collections of these questions and answers, known as responsa, are presented in this chapter for you to study.

Responsum Written by Solomon ben Adret. *Rome, 1469.*

The Need for Responsa

In each generation Jews have worked to bring Jewish law into their lives. But what happened when circumstances arose that were not directly mentioned in the *Mishnah*, *Gemara*, their commentaries, or the codes? Or what if someone were not familiar enough with these texts to know how to find the answer to a question? At these times, the questioner turned to especially respected rabbis and asked for clarification of the *halachah* ("Jewish law") on a given topic. As new questions arose, new responsa would be written. Not surprisingly, the process of writing responsa continues to the present.

The format of responsa is quite simple. The question is stated, and the answer is given. Sometimes the question comes from an individual Jew; other times a whole Jewish community may have a question. As you study the following examples of responsa, think about the ways the questions touch your daily life and how you would respond to them.

Must He Obey His Father?

Rabbi Asher ben Yechiel was born in Germany around 1250 and died in Toledo, Spain, in 1327. He wrote the following responsum. This responsum answers whether or not there are times *not* to follow the *mitzvah* ("commandment") "You shall revere your mother and father . . . ." (*Vayikra*/Leviticus 19:3)

Question: A father told his son not to speak to a certain Jew and not to forgive him for what he had done. The son would like to patch things up but he is concerned about his father's command. What should the son do?

Answer: Let me make it clear that . . . the father who told his son to hate this Jew had no right to order his son to violate a Torah decree. The verse "You shall revere your mother and father. . . " concludes with the words "I *Adonai* am your God," which indicates that God's law must be obeyed even if a parent tells you to violate it. Besides, by giving such an order, the father was acting in an un-Jewish manner. This being so, the son is not required to obey the father. (*Teshuvot* Rabbi Asher ben Yechiel, No. 15:5)

ACTIVITIES

Which of the following do you think best describes the message of the above responsum? Put a check in front of your choice.

_____ 1. When a child does not agree with his/her parent, the child is correct in disobeying the parent.

_____ 2. The Torah teaches us that we are commanded to revere and honor our parents. The Torah also teaches us that we have an even greater responsibility to revere and honor God.

_____ 3. Only in the case described in this responsum is a child allowed not to follow the commandment to "revere your mother and father."

Using this responsum as a guide, describe another situation in which a child would not be obligated to obey the commandment "You shall revere your mother and father . . . ."

_____

_____

_____

Visiting the Sick by Telephone

The following responsum was written by Rabbi Yonaton Steif, who was born in Czechoslovakia in 1877. After miraculously escaping the Nazis during World War II, he came to America where he lived until his death in 1958. This responsum is an example of how modern technology can pose new questions for *halachah*. The *mitzvah* of *Bikur Cholim*, "visiting the sick," which we discussed in the last chapter on the *Shulchan Aruch*, is the topic of this responsum.

Question: Do you fulfill the *mitzvah* of *Bikur Cholim*, "visiting the sick," by calling the patient on the telephone?

Answer: There is no doubt that calling a sick person on the telephone is considered visiting the sick person. Rambam classifies the *mitzvah* of visiting the sick under the heading of "loving your neighbor." This being the case, any favor you do for your friend, even if you do it by telephone, is a manifestation of "loving your neighbor." Nevertheless, the essential *mitzvah* of visiting the sick should be done by personally going to see the patient. Seeing the patient's suffering will stir your feelings more than merely talking to the person on the telephone. It will cause you to pray more fervently for the person, and you will see more clearly what the needs of the person are. . . . (*Teshuvot* Rabbi Yonaton Steif, No. 294)

| **ACTIVITIES** |

Based on this responsum, write a "T" next to those statements that are true and an "F" next to those that are false.

_____ Calling a sick person on the phone fulfills the *mitzvah* of *Bikur Cholim.*

_____ It is preferable to visit sick people face to face rather than to call them on the phone.

_____ In addition to visiting sick people, we are obligated to pray for their recovery.

_____ If you call a sick person and the person is unable to come to the phone, it is still considered fulfilling the *mitzvah* of *Bikur Cholim.*

After reading this responsum, do you think that sending someone a videotaped message would be considered as fulfilling the *mitzvah* of *Bikur Cholim*? _____

Complete: I think that a videotape message (would/would not) fulfill this *mitzvah* because _____

_____

Modern Reform Responsa

As pointed out earlier, responsa continue to be written to this day. In a collection called *Contemporary American Reform Responsa*, edited by Walter Jacob , we find responsa written by contemporary Reform rabbis. A few samples follow.

Dress Codes

Question: Our religious school has insisted on a dress code for young people both in religious school and, especially, for attendance at synagogue services. Is there anything in Jewish tradition that points to "proper attire" for attendance at synagogue services?

Answer: The question may be restated as follows: Does the Jewish tradition give the synagogue community or the rabbis the right to make rules about proper dress? The first part of our answer is that we find that such legislation began as early as the times of the *Mishnah*.

Restrictions applicable to synagogue services became frequent in the Middle Ages. Many of these restrictions represented concern that extravagant dress could cause envy by non-Jews. For example, the decrees passed at Forli, Italy, in 1416, dealt with and warned against extravagant dress worn in public. While many decrees dealt with women's dress, a wide variety of medieval sources also mention curbing extravagant clothing of men.

A discussion of special garments to be worn on the Sabbath appears in the Talmud (*Shabbat* 113a) and declares that those who possess a change of clothing should wear the new clothing on the Sabbath, and those who do not simply should make the old clothing look a little better, in order to honor the Sabbath. The point of this passage is to assure that the Sabbath is distinguished from other days in every possible way, "dress, speech, manner of walking, etc."

In terms of decrees concerned specifically with dress in the synagogue, there is a medieval decree dealing with the problem of dirt caused by wooden shoes worn in the synagogue and prohibited them inside the building.

We can see from these points and other sources that might be cited that rabbinic authorities had the authority to regulate dress within and outside the synagogue. Certainly, this would have been used to assure the proper attire had such laws been necessary. A modern rabbi must also insist that dress in the synagogue be appropriate but also not too flashy.

(March 1976)

ACTIVITIES

According to your understanding of the above responsum, fill in the chart below.

Item	Acceptable Dress for Synagogue	Unacceptable Dress for Synagogue
dirty sneakers baseball hats a skirt and blouse an evening gown torn jeans a shirt and slacks gardening shoes a coat and tie		

Write a dress code for your religious school. Include categories of clothing that would be allowed and categories of those that would not be allowed. _____

_____

_____

Videotaping in the Synagogue

Question: Is there any objection to videotaping a bar/bat mitzvah at a service or a wedding ceremony?

Answer: The custom of videotaping family celebrations in the synagogue has grown in recent years. We would generally discourage it as it is often intrusive. However, videotaping does provide a permanent family record of notable occasions in an individual's life. Furthermore, it often enables individuals who are too old or frail to witness the ceremony to do so at home or in the hospital.

Videotaping can be less intrusive than the earlier use of photography. [But it is important to remember that] we have always considered it important to maintain the proper behavior at the synagogue service, both public services and private occasions like weddings. A variety of Jewish texts remind us that nothing may distract the worshiper from worship. (Talmud, *Megillah* 28a; Rambam's *Mishneh Torah, Hilchot Tefilah* 6; *Shulchan Aruch, Orah Hayim* 151.1) It is, therefore, essential to keep the videotaping as a recording of what has occurred and not "stage" the service for the taping. The latter is not acceptable to us. If the videotaping can be done without interfering with the flow of the service and be invisible to the majority of the congregation, it is permissible.

(November 1986)

ACTIVITY

Which of the situations below describes the use of videotaping that follows the opinion of this responsum? Check as many as you think are correct.

_____ 1. at a wedding having the videophotographer under the *chupah* with the bride and groom

_____ 2. at a bar/bat mitzvah having the videophotographer sitting in the first row

_____ 3. at a bar/bat mitzvah having the videophotographer standing in a corner in the back of the sanctuary

_____ 4. at a wedding having the videophotographer up in the balcony where no one is sitting

Page from a Siddur: The Shabbat Evening Service. *Italian, 1460-1470.*

Siddur as Responsa

A most amazing and possibly surprising example of responsa is the *siddur* ("prayer book"). How did this come about? Throughout our history Jews prayed. During the times that the Temple stood in Jerusalem, most prayers were connected to sacrifices. Once the Temple was destroyed (both in 586 B.C.E. and in 70 C.E.), Jews continued to gather together to pray. Some prayers from the Temple services were remembered and kept alive. To these were added new prayers, poems, and songs. Over time a structure began to develop for Jewish prayer services.

It was not until the 800s C.E. that the first true prayer book was organized by the great Babylonian scholar Rav Amram Gaon. Rav Amram Gaon received a series of questions about prayers and worship services from Jews living in Spain. In response to their questions Rav Amram Gaon laid out an organized approach to prayer. His *siddur* became the foundation for all future Jewish prayer books. Throughout the centuries that followed, additions and expansions have been made to the *siddur*, but the basic format has remained the same. Today, if you go into any synagogue in the world, you will find that the organization of the service is essentially the same as the service in your home temple.

In many ways the *siddur* may be viewed as a compilation of excerpts from most of the sacred texts we have studied in this book. There are many sections taken from the Torah, including the words of the *Shema* and the *Veahavta* (*Devarim* 6:4-9) and the song *Mi Chamochah* (*Shemot* 15:11). Of course, every Shabbat we read selections from the Torah and *Nevi'im* ("the Prophets"). In addition, every service includes selections from the Book of Psalms, which you remember are found in *Ketuvim* ("the Writings"). There are also selections from the *Mishnah* and Talmud, as well as a wide range of poems and songs written by rabbis over the ages, included in the *siddur*.

From all this we learn that prayer and study are very closely connected. Praying is a form of studying and learning for, as we listen and recite the words of prayer, we think about their meanings and importance. And studying Jewish texts is a form of giving thanks to God for by studying texts we acknowledge their importance to generations of Jews, and we help to keep both the Jewish people and our texts alive.

Our Sacred Texts: Summary

Congratulations! You have now completed the study of our sacred texts. You have come a long way since you were first introduced to the two stories about Jews who risked their lives to study Jewish texts. You explored the *Tanach*, starting with the Torah, the Five Books of Moses. You examined and commented on selected readings from each of the five books. You found that certain key themes are repeated throughout the Torah, especially the importance of the *berit* between God and the Jewish people. Next you studied *Nevi'im*, "the Prophets," where you encountered the establishment of the monarchy to rule over and guide the Jewish people. You also learned about the role of the prophet as the social conscience. You finished your *Tanach* studies with *Ketuvim*, "the Writings," where you were introduced to examples of the poetry of the Book of Psalms and the wisdom of the Book of Proverbs.

After the *Tanach*, you ventured into the world of rabbinic literature. You learned the difference between Oral Law and Written Law. You successfully tackled difficult selections from the *Mishnah* and Talmud. And you followed the example of the authors of *midrashim* and tried to write your own. You moved on to learning about codes of Jewish law and how they cover every aspect of the life of a Jew. Finally, in this chapter you discovered yet another collection of texts that helps Judaism expand, grow, and evolve. You saw how responsa, like all sacred texts, have developed as a way to keep Judaism up to date and in touch with the changing needs of each generation.

Throughout this textbook you have been challenged to turn our sacred texts into texts that have meaning for you today. By discovering personal meaning in the selections in this textbook, you have not only learned *about* our sacred texts, but you also have become a part of the process of keeping them alive and lively. So long as Jews continue to know about, to read, and to study our sacred texts, Judaism will live on from generation to generation.